Uncovering Hidden Treasures:

Practical Bible Study Methods by Example

Samuel C. Tseng

WestBow
PRESS
A DIVISION OF THOMAS NELSON

WestBow Press books may be ordered through booksellers or by contacting:

WestBow Press
A Division of Thomas Nelson
1663 Liberty Drive
Bloomington, IN 47403
www.westbowpress.com
1-(866) 928-1240

ISBN: 978-1-4497-1276-1 (sc)
ISBN: 978-1-4497-1277-8 (dj)
ISBN: 978-1-4497-1275-4 (e)

Library of Congress Control Number: 2001012345

Printed in the United States of America

WestBow Press rev. date: 04/08/2011

Contents

Preface

❧

Though born into a Buddhist family, I became an atheist during my undergraduate college days, believing only in physics and math. Later, while I was in graduate school, God extended His mercy to me, and I received Jesus Christ as my Lord and Savior. That was fifty years ago.

My experience with Bible reading progressed by stages: first, with a rebellious and skeptical mind; second, as a routine Christian duty that lacked excitement; and finally, I found myself gratefully enjoying meditation[1] on the Scripture. These experiences were invaluable to me as I served the Lord by teaching adult Sunday school at four churches during the past twenty-five years.

---

1   In this book, the terms *meditation* and *reflection* are loosely interchangeable. In *Merriam-Webster's 11th Collegiate Dictionary*, *reflection* is defined as "a thought, idea, or opinion formed, or a remark made as a result of meditation."

The title of this book, *Uncovering Hidden Treasures* (quoting Matthew 13:44), may sound as if it is one of those how-to-study books, but it is more about sharing my personal reflection on various passages in the Scripture. I'm praying that readers will benefit from the Bible study methods that I use in this book.

Many authors have written excellent books that help a person study the Bible, such as:

1. Rick Warren, *Bible Study Methods*, Zondervan, 2006.

2. H. G. Hendricks and W. D. Hendricks, *Living by the Book*, Moody Press, 1991.

3. E. W. Bullinger (1837–1913), *How to Enjoy the Bible*, Kregel Classics, 1990.

Warren's book is subtitled: *Twelve Ways You Can Unlock God's Word*. Bullinger's book is subtitled: *Twelve Basic Principles for Understanding God's Word*. But readers should not expect to find one-to-one mapping (or correspondence) between these two sets of twelve canons.

Each of the three authors has his own organization, emphasis, and style of presenting his teaching. However, the teaching in all three books can best be summarized by the three steps in the Hendricks book:

a) *Observation*—Careful and exhaustive observation should generate many questions.

b) *Interpretation*—Seek answers to these questions by interpreting Scripture. Make sure to correlate[2] your new insights or findings with scriptures that you know.

c) *Application*—Apply the Bible truths to your daily life.

The rest of the rules are details for helping readers carry out the above three steps. Methods and rules are important, and I am sure these books have helped many people. However, my twenty-five years of experience in adult Sunday school tells me that there are two types of students: (1) Some students believe that God was *testing* Abraham's loyalty by demanding the sacrifice of Isaac, for the Bible *explicitly* says so. (2) Other students also believe what the Bible says as in (1), but they further believe that God wanted Abraham to experience sorrow and agony beyond description when he had to sacrifice his beloved son Isaac. These students believe that God wants all people to know, through our empathy for Abraham's feeling, how much He loves His Son, Jesus, and appreciate the deeper truth that God so loved the world that He had to give His only begotten Son to save our souls.

I found that students of the first type follow the how-to-study books diligently, but the others are not anxious to learn rigorous definitions, principles, and methodologies. Instead they want to

---

2   Warren emphasizes that the student must correlate his discovery or new insights with scriptures he knows during his study. There are new insights to be found.

see examples of how the methods are applied and then figure out the methods. I believe the authors of the aforementioned books must once have been the second type of students and later developed the principles and methods.[3] I have adopted a different approach in this book. Instead of defining and explaining the principles and methods, I have meditated on various passages in an attempt to answer the questions brought up by Christians, seekers, and skeptics. In the process, I have pointed out a few keys that might help these persons meditate on their own.

So, how did I select the passages in this book? I used the following criteria:

- Passages that often generate questions by adult Sunday school teachers, students, and bloggers who discuss the Christian faith online.

- Passages which are already familiar to new believers and so familiar to mature Christians that they think no insight remains there to be found.

- Passages in which I believe I have uncovered *hidden treasures* to enhance our faith, thus proving that the following statements are true:

---

3   In the Preface of his book *Bible Study Methods*, Warren says that he was first motivated by good sermons or in-depth Bible teaching, and then he developed all these methods.

The idea here is to do whatever it takes to see the Word from a different perspective.... What a tragedy, especially when we consider that history's greatest works of art and music have been created by people who learned to read the Bible imaginatively.—by H. G. Hendricks and W. D. Hendricks[4]

Don't let someone else rob you of the joy of discovering biblical insights on your own. Never let reading a commentary take the place of your personal Bible study.—by Rick Warren[5]

[There are] some biblical truths that I believe have been long ignored or spiritualized and thereby stripped of their richness and significance.—by Randy Alcorn[6]

I also believe that people cannot know God's will unless He reveals it to them, and He reveals only as much as they can absorb. As civilization progresses, the Holy Spirit will give additional insight and clarity from the same passages of the Scripture. Thus, in chapters 6 through 9, I have employed discoveries

---

4   Howard G. Hendricks and William D. Hendricks, *Living by the Book* (Chicago: Moody Press, 1991), 107.

5   Rick Warren, *Bible Study Methods* (Grand Rapids: Zondervan, 2006), 27.

6   Randy Alcorn, *Heaven* (Tyndale, 2004), Preface, xiv .

in science and engineering to support several hard-to-explain theological topics. For example, in the narrative of the first two days of the Creation, the Scripture has clearly told us that light has finite speed and the universe is finite and expanding. These facts have never been mentioned in books written by scientists who are believers, to the author's knowledge.

Recently, the faith of many Christians and seekers has been shaken by statements of the renowned physicist Stephen Hawking in a new book and in the interview by ABC anchorwoman Diane Sawyer. Hawking stated that God does not need to be involved for the creation of the universe to take place. In chapter 10, I offer several observations opposing this view and advise readers not to worship science or the scientists and keep hold of their faith in God.

In addition, I illustrate that many problems cannot be solved or explained by quantitative analysis of physics or math and that their solution must rely on metaphysics. When metaphysics is involved, the distinction between science and religion fades, and they converge on questions that are resolved by faith in God.

Unless otherwise specified, scripture quotations are from the *New American Standard Bible*. Quotations marked NIV are from the New International Version, those marked NLT from the New Living Translation.[7]

I prayerfully hope that the readers of this book will be encouraged to dig a little deeper into the Bible to find the hidden treasures—the Way, the Truth, and the Life in the Word of God.

Samuel C. Tseng

June 2010

---

7   NEW AMERICAN STANDARD BIBLE, copyright 1960, 1962, 1963, 1968, 1971, 1972, 1973, 1975, 1977, 1995 by The Lockman Foundation. All rights Reserved. Used by permission. HOLY BIBLE: NEW INTERNATIONAL VERSION, copyright 1973, 1978, 1984 International Bible Society; used by permission of Zondervan Bible Publishers. HOLY BIBLE, NEW LIVING TRANSLATION, copyright 1996. Used by permission of Tyndale House Publishers, Inc. All rights reserved.

Acknowledgment

Thanks to Pastor Jay Thompson; Janice Tsai, MD; and Jennifer Tseng for reviewing parts of my manuscript.

To Eleanor Chen, an adult Sunday school teacher, who constantly brings me challenging questions about the Christian faith that she has found online and elsewhere.

To Paul Hawley, at Believerspress.com, who not only edited the manuscript but checked Scripture references and offered comments and queries on matters of interpretation. I highly recommend his services to anyone writing about the Christian faith.

1. Do You Wish to Get Well?
A Deeper Look at John 5:2–9

Why did Jesus heal just one and not all people at the pool of Bethesda?

Answer: He did heal many! Do not just see the individual trees and miss the forest.

When a pastor I most respect and admire for his dynamic preaching wrote a book about the power to heal, he said, "While the Lord Jesus often healed a multitude of sick people, He only healed one person at the pool of Bethesda. He left the others sick." The pastor's explanation was that the Lord exercised His sovereign will.[8]

I cannot agree more so far as the following truths are concerned: the Lord Jesus has absolute sovereign will. He will do what He wants to do, when He wants to do it, and He cannot be forced to do it (Exod. 33:19). However, I *also* believe that

---

8   John Hagee, *The Power to Heal* (Boerne, TX: Rudkin Production, 1991), 7.

it is not the nature of the Lord Jesus to refuse a person who humbly comes to Him for help with *extraordinary faith* in Him. This is shown in the case of Jesus healing the woman who hemorrhaged for twelve years (Mark 5:25–34). She did not even ask the Lord's will.

Jesus told a parable about a bad judge and a widow in Luke 18:1–7, in which He taught people to pray and not to lose heart. Even a bad judge would give in to a widow's persistent petition, so how could a merciful heavenly Father refuse to help His children? Unlike the bad judge, I believe it is not that the Lord God is coerced by persistent prayers, but He is responding to His children's petition willingly with love and compassion in His *own way.*

Clearly, it all depends on the angle from which a reader of the Bible views the multiple facets of God's many attributes. Thus, let us reflect on this passage from a different perspective.

If the Lord Jesus did not heal all, there had to be simple explanations. To begin, let us compare the case of Bethesda in the gospel of John with the following two verses in Matthew.

> The news about Him spread throughout all Syria; and they brought to Him all who were ill, those suffering with various diseases and pains, demoniacs, epileptics, paralytics; and He healed them. (Matt. 4:24)

When evening came, they brought to Him many who were demon-possessed; and He cast out the spirits with a word, and healed all who were ill. (Matt. 8:16)

Please note the words "healed them" and "healed all" in the above two passages. Also, note a decisively crucial factor, namely that the above-mentioned people came to Jesus with faith. In the case of Bethesda, the sick people did not come to the Lord Jesus; it was He who visited them, just as He visited us sinners from heaven to declare the good news—salvation by faith in Him. He could save the souls of all humankind, but He saves only those who believe in Him.

About the healing at Bethesda, the Scripture says:

Now there is in Jerusalem by the sheep gate a pool, which is called in Hebrew Bethesda, having five porticoes. In these lay a multitude of those who were sick, blind, lame, and withered, [waiting for the moving of the waters; for an angel of the Lord went down at certain seasons into the pool and stirred up the water; whoever then first, after the stirring up of the water, stepped in was made well from whatever disease with which he was afflicted.] A man was there who had been ill for thirty-eight years. When Jesus saw him lying

3

there, and knew that he had already been a long time in that condition, He said to him, "Do you wish to get well?" The sick man answered Him, "Sir, I have no man to put me into the pool when the water is stirred up, but while I am coming, another steps down before me." Jesus said to him, "Get up, pick up your pallet and walk." Immediately the man became well, and picked up his pallet and began to walk.

Now it was the Sabbath on that day. (John 5:2–9)

Having Five Porticoes

Some Bible scholars and teachers have quoted a view found in earlier works that the five porticoes represent the first five books of the Jewish Scriptures (i.e., the Pentateuch).[9] I do not know whether the architect had that concept in mind or not when he designed that five-portico structure, but we can imagine how large the size of the pool was, and therefore, the size of the multitude of sick and handicapped people resting around the pool.

Verse 4 describes the people's belief of that time. They believed that an angel would come and occasionally stir up

---

9   William MacDonald (Art Farstad, ed.), *Believer's Bible Commentary* (Thomas Nelson Publishers, 1995); Herbert Lockyer, *All the Miracles of The Bible* (Zondervan, 1961), 166.

the water. They also believed that at the moment the water was stirred, the first person to jump into the pool would be cured of the disease[10]. The description seems to say that the water had no healing power for the second person who went into the water. Also, it does not say what would happen if two persons jumped in the pool at the same time when the water was stirred up. We can come up with many possibilities:

- It may be the act of an angel, or it may be the underground flow of water mixed with air bubbles or change in water pressure from time to time that caused the water to stir up.

- The healing power of the water might just be a superstition, or the stirred-up water might contain some minerals coming up from the bottom of the pool that could cure certain diseases. We do not have the exact answer, because the Bible doesn't say.

The Lord's Question: "Do You Wish to Get Well?"

Verses 5–6 say that Jesus took pity on a man who had been ill for thirty-eight years and asked him, "Do you wish to get well?" The question may sound superfluous to some people, for they figure, who in his or her right mind wouldn't want to get well?

---

10 *The NIV Study Bible* (Zondervan), note at John 5:3–4; Walvoord and Zuck, *Bible Knowledge Commentary N.T.*

In order to make sense out of the Lord Jesus' question, some teachers give a possible interpretation that disabled persons do not necessarily wish to get well in many cases, because they do not have to work while they are ill. The interpretation concludes that the Lord Jesus asked that question in order to know this man's real wish.[11] Such a conclusion may have stemmed from the fact that the invalid man did not directly answer yes or no to the question. Thus some Bible students may have concluded that he was evading the question to cover up his laziness. However, this explanation cannot be satisfactory, for he still wanted to fight to be the first to get into the pool. Thus his answer *implied* that he wanted to get healed.

The Lord's question is not superfluous at all. This person had been ill for thirty-eight years. The illness was incurable. If it could be cured, it would have been cured by an ordinary human physician long before. Because he had given up all hope in human ability to cure him, he came to the pool seeking a miracle as the last resort.

So let us look at this conversation from three different perspectives.

(1) Imagine an ordinary person coming to this man and asking the same question: "Do you wish to get well?" Assume this sick man's answer was yes. What do you think would have happened? Nothing!

---

11 William Barclay, *The Gospel of John*, vol. 1 (Westminster Press, 1956), 179. This book also gives another possible reason: the man might have given up all hope to get well.

No one could heal him, and nothing had happened for the past thirty-eight years. Therefore, if the question was asked by an ordinary man, then the question would be superfluous. But it makes eminent sense for the Lord Jesus to ask him; in fact, only He is qualified to ask that question.

The Lord never wastes words. Every one of His words has purpose. Similar to this case in Bethesda, only the Lord Jesus is qualified to tell Nicodemus to be born again (John 3:1–3). Only the Lord Jesus is qualified to offer the Samaritan woman the water that will well up to eternal life (John 4:10- 14). These were the Lord's evangelistic approaches to save individuals, and He chose the right words at the right place and time, according to each individual's need, background, and circumstances. (Here is a lesson for us to learn in leading people to faith.)

Thus, I believe the question, "Do you wish to get well?" cannot be an exception. It has purposes when the Lord uses it. It may sound as if it is just a question lightly asking about the wish of this person, but I believe it can also have a hidden meaning declaring the power of the Lord as, *"Nobody could make you well in the past thirty-eight years, but I can. Do you wish to get well?"* It implies that the person who asked the question is the Son of God, who has the supernatural power to cure the incurable. Is it superfluous? No!

(2) The omnipotent Lord can heal any afflictions, but the receiving party must have faith in Him. In Mark 9:20–25, the Lord

demanded faith, when a father begged Jesus to heal his demon-possessed son. The father had a tone of doubt in his request:

> "It [the evil spirit] has often thrown him both into the fire and into the water to destroy him. But if You can do anything, take pity on us and help us!" And Jesus said to him, "'If You can?' All things are possible to him who believes." Immediately the boy's father cried out and said, "I do believe; help my unbelief." (Mark 9:22–24)

In response to the father's uncertain faith, "If You can do anything ..."— the Lord repeated the father's question, "If You can?"[12] (Note the capital letter in "You" referring to the Lord in NASB.) The father of the demon-possessed young man did not have complete faith in the Lord, did he? Therefore, in the case of the paralytic man at Bethesda, I believe the Lord is also challenging this invalid to have faith in Him. The question could be, "Do you wish to get well? *If you do, believe in Me.*"

Such an inference is not unfounded, for even to His disciples the Lord said, "Do not let your heart be troubled; believe in God, believe also in Me" (John 14:1). He demanded faith of all His followers.

---

12 The question mark is added to the New American Standard Bible and the New International Version, as compared to the King James Version, so as to make verse 24 clearer.

Why didn't the Lord Jesus just say it clearly? Again I believe the Lord had His reasons, and it is for us to uncover the hidden treasure.

(3) Imagine a psychiatrist and a patient in a session for mental treatment. The doctor never asks a long and complicated question. Instead, he asks a simple question, but the question is enough to bring out the patient's thoughts that are buried deep inside the patient's mind. In this sense, the Lord Jesus plausibly succeeded. By a simple question, He was able to make this man pour out his soul to Him. The invalid man said, "Sir, I have no man to put me into the pool when the water is stirred up, but while I am coming, another steps down before me" (John 5:7). This man's answer released his innermost feelings of bitterness, hatred, frustration, and resentment toward other people and his self-pity, misery, helplessness, and hopelessness toward himself:

- Why me? Why would God let me suffer like this for thirty-eight years?

- Why does the angel only heal the first one to jump into the pool; why not heal all?

- Why doesn't anybody care about me?

- Why are people so selfish, pushing other people aside, even stampeding weaker people to fight to be the first to jump in the pool?

(Haven't we all asked similar questions in our life at one time or another?)

The Scripture says, "A joyful heart is good medicine, but a broken spirit dries up the bones." (Prov. 17:22) When the Lord Jesus asked, "Do you wish to get well?" He knew He had to restore this man's broken spirit first, by making him let out all the bitterness in his heart. Jesus cures from the root of the disease. The Lord Jesus knew what He was doing by asking one short and simple question. As a result, He healed the man's spirit and mind as well as his body.

This man did not come to Jesus with faith; it was Jesus who initiated the conversation. (Could there be a lesson here? Perhaps the Lord is teaching us that we as Christians should share about Him with unbelievers and that we should be the ones to initiate the conversation.)

In verse 8, the Lord then exercised His divine authority to command the thirty-eight years of affliction to leave this person with a word that was as simple as His question was. His authority and power made the illness and the man obey His command instantly without any resistance. May His name be praised!

Jesus Healed Only One Man (?)

Now we have come to the question of why Jesus did not heal all, but just singled out that person who had been ill for thirty-eight years. On the contrary, I claim that Jesus did not just heal one person. I will elaborate on this later.

A preacher I know interpreted that Jesus always has mercy on the weakest and the most hopeless person. That may be true, but such an interpretation makes new seekers and skeptics think that Jesus is unfair. And if the word *unfair* is mentioned, the preacher would say that the Lord has the sovereign power to do whatever He pleases. In this regard, I believe the Lord Jesus loves and cares about all people with compassion, not necessarily only the weakest. The best example is that the Lord loved and saved the soul of Zacchaeus, too. Zacchaeus might have been short, but he was never weak. He was a chief tax collector—powerful in his community—and wealthy (Luke 19:1–2). I believe there are many reasons for Jesus to just single out this one man at this particular situation.

John 5:9 clearly states that "it was the Sabbath on that day." If He had stayed there to heal the entire multitude, it would have caused a big commotion. Healing people on the Sabbath was one of the reasons the Jewish rulers decided to kill the Lord Jesus (Mark 3:1–6; John 5:18). It was not time for Jesus to get public attention, because His time to die on the cross was yet to come. Thus Jesus slipped away into the crowd (v. 13).

The man had been ill for thirty-eight years, meaning that he had a disease which no physician at the time could treat by human abilities. By healing this man, Jesus demonstrated to the rest of the people lying around the pool that He could heal every one of them too, because their illnesses were not as severe as this man's. On the other hand, if Jesus had selected and healed a man with a less severe illness, this person with an incurable disease might not necessarily believe that Jesus was able to heal him, and still kept his eyes on the water. Thus, the Lord Jesus singled out this man, the most severely afflicted— and not because Jesus just cares about the weakest.

Once the multitude witnessed the healing of this man, I am sure the multitude would be divided into two groups of people:

- One group had no faith in Christ and would still be lying around waiting for the water to stir up; they would still be unbelievers even if they witnessed the resurrection of a dead man (Luke 16:31).

- The other group would recognize the real healer and look for Jesus to help. These people would eventually leave the pool and come looking for Jesus with *faith* as those people described in Matthew 4:24 and 8:16, the two verses quoted at the beginning of this chapter.

In conclusion, the Lord Jesus did not heal just one, but healed *all those who believed in Him and eventually left the pool and came to Him.* I believe this is one implicit treasure that has been overlooked by many in this passage.

A critic has commented that my statement is merely a conjecture, a guess that some of the people would leave the pool and seek Jesus for healing, because the Scripture does not explicitly say so. However, it is precisely the point, in order to dig deeper for treasures that are not explicit on the surface Hendricks teaches that one should read the Bible passages imaginatively.[13]

To me it is not a conjecture; it is real to my *life*. I was an atheist believing that wealth, career, and physical health (my pool of Bethesda) were the only security and salvation. Then I saw changes in my mother and elder sister who were once devoted Buddhists (like the man in affliction for thirty-eight years) and converted to become Christians (picked up their pallet and began to walk). Their testimonies made me rethink the value of life (leave the pool of Bethesda), and I decided to follow my Savior Jesus.

Summary and Application

I believe these reflections from a different perspective compared to the traditional commentaries have led us to find hidden treasures.

- The Lord's question, "Do you wish to get well?" makes a lot of sense to initiate the process of healing the patient's spirit and mind as well as his body. The

---

13 H. G. Hendricks and W. D. Hendricks, *Living by the Book* (Chicago: Moody Press, 1991), 103.

same question is now directed to us sinners as well: "Do you wish to be *saved*?"

- With this question, He is telling us that He has the authority and power to save, and He demands our answer with "faith" to His call.

- Healing the most severely afflicted sick man was the Lord Jesus' call to all people. His victory over death (the most severe affliction) is His call directed to all human races to believe in Him as the One and only Savior (Acts 4:12).

- Those who believed Him and left the pool to seek their Savior were the wise ones in response to His call. The Lord is calling for our decision to confess our faith.

- We must ask ourselves which group we are in now. Do we still doubt Jesus and stay, waiting for the water to stir up, or do we trust and obey Him and pick up our own pallet and walk?

- The Bible says in John 5:15, "The man went away and told the Jews that it was Jesus who had made him well." This passage calls for our witnessing to share Jesus with our family, friends, and whoever else does not yet know Him.

- When facing problems in life, let us not just concentrate on the problem itself, but look for the solution, and remember that the Lord Jesus Christ said, "Come to me, all you who are weary and burdened, and I will give you rest." (Matt. 11:28, NIV)

2. Jesus and the Fig Tree
A Different Perspective on Mark 11

—❧—

Even though a Bible passage ultimately has only one correct interpretation, you'll always find two Christians who disagree about what that interpretation ought to be ... Differences in interpretation are fine as long as we keep in mind that the conflict is not in the text, but in our limited understanding of the text.

—Hendricks, *Living by the Book* (Moody Press, 1991), 207.

I find the above statement to be true. Even Bible scholars have different interpretations of the same passages. For example, there are at least three different interpretations that I know about how the Lord Jesus got the colt to ride into Jerusalem (Mark 11:1–6):

a) Jesus had made prearranged plans with the colt's owner.[14]

b) Jesus exercised His supernatural power of foreknowledge and complete authority over the owner as well as the unbroken colt.[15]

c) The Lord said, "If anyone asks you ...." The message concerning the colt was not directed specifically to the owner but to anyone who might question the disciples' action. Thus, the footnote in the *NIV Study Bible*[16] seems to say that the name and the work of the Lord were well known by then, and therefore the Lord did not have to prearrange with the owner.

Even more differing opinions, suggestions, and interpretations exist regarding the passages on Jesus and the fig tree.[17] The Scripture says:

---

14 William Barclay, *The Daily Study Bible Series* (Westminster Press, 1975).
15 William MacDonald and Art L. Farstad, *Believer's Bible Commentary* (Thomas Nelson, 1990)
16 *NIV Study Bible*, footnote at Mark 11:3.
17 http://www.christiancourier.com/articles/646-why-did-jesus-curse-the-fig-tree
http://atheism.about.com/od/biblegospelofmark/a/mark11b.html
http://home.earthlink.net/~ronrhodes/qtreecursed.html
http://www.tektonics.org/uz/zapfigtree.html, "Was Jesus Being Unreasonable When He Zapped the Fig Tree?"

> On the next day, when they had left Bethany, He became hungry. Seeing at a distance a fig tree in leaf, He went to see if perhaps He would find anything on it; and when He came to it, He found nothing but leaves, for it was not the season for figs. He said to it, "May no one ever eat fruit from you again!" And His disciples were listening. (Mark 11:12–14)

The skeptics and even some bona fide seekers typically interpret this passage literally and conclude that Jesus got hungry, He saw a fig tree, He approached the tree, He looked for fruit, and He could not find any, so He got angry and cursed and killed the tree. He was demanding the tree to bear fruit when it was not the season for figs, and so He was unreasonable.

The answers by believers to the above misguided conclusion vary, but all seem to have in common the following two aspects:

- The fig tree is a symbol for the nation of Israel. Figs as symbols for Israel appear several times in the Old Testament, (e.g., Jeremiah 24:1–9; Hosea 9:10).

- Jesus' cursing of the fig tree, which has leaves but bears no fruit, is in fact His accusation of the people of Israel for their outwardly religious appearance but with spiritual barrenness in their hearts.

These two core interpretations are typically padded with explanations, attempting to correct a skeptic's misunderstanding of the Lord.

In this chapter, I offer my own personal reflections, viewing the passages from an entirely different perspective. My interpretations of this passage are different from those of other believers, but I am, just like any other Christian, only attempting to get as close as possible to the meaning intended by the Lord. The one ultimate correct interpretation has to wait until the time when we can humbly ask the Lord before His glorious throne.

Did Jesus Exercise His Divine Power?

On the Christian Courier website, an article, "Why Did Jesus Curse the Fig Tree?" by Wayne Jackson, says the following:

> When the Lord first saw the tree, he was yet afar off. He could only discern that it had leaves (v. 13). One must conclude that this circumstance reveals that though He was deity, Jesus did not exercise the full range of His divine powers constantly; He did not know the details regarding this tree until He was in close proximity (v. 13b).[18]

---

18 http://www.christiancourier.com/articles/646-why-did-jesus-curse-the-fig-tree

Although every person is entitled to draw his own conclusion on a passage of the Bible, my understanding of the same verse is that this is Mark's narration of the Lord's act *observed* by His disciples, and it does not reveal how much the Lord knew or how much He did not know.

Let us consider the following:

- In verse 13, the Scripture clearly states that it was *not* the season for figs, and it strains credulity to maintain that Jesus did not know it.

- According to Walvoord and Zuck[19] and documents quoted by them, the fig trees produce small buds in the middle of March, followed by the appearance of green leaves in April. For a fruitful tree, the buds will grow into fruits, but for a barren tree these buds will drop off. Thus the tree that the Lord and His disciples saw could have already been in bud but barren; at least there was that possibility.

- In Matthew 21:19, the tree is described as "a lone fig tree by the road." Jackson explains that this tree did not have an owner, and therefore Jesus did not destroy anyone's property. In my opinion, that argument goes far in answering any objection to the Lord's act of destroying someone's tree.

---

19 *Bible Knowledge Commentary N.T.*

However, I would also conclude that it was precisely because the tree was by the road without an owner that it was so undernourished that it became barren. The Lord tells a parable in Luke 13:6–9, in which a man planted a fig tree in a vineyard. Since the fig tree did not bear fruit for three years,[20] he wanted to cut it down. But the man who took care of the vineyard suggested waiting another year and said, "I'll dig around it and fertilize it." (Luke 13:8, NIV) Certainly, digging around a tree and fertilizing it are necessary practices for any fig tree to bear fruit. Now, this lone tree was by the roadside, meaning the earth around it must have been hard. Because it had no caretaker to fertilize it, the tree was more likely to be barren.

In Mark 13:28–29, the Lord gave another parable. Verse 28 (NIV) says, "Now learn this lesson from the fig tree: As soon as its twigs get tender and its leaves come out, you know that summer is near." Aside from His predictions of the rebirth of the nation of Israel[21] and His second coming, this verse tells us that when it is spring, not only is summer near, but also spring is the time that twigs of a fig tree get tender and its young leaves *just start* to emerge. We know that the fig tree by the roadside that the Lord and His disciples saw was a *leafy* tree, because they could see the leaves from a distance; and that it was sometime

---

20 Could the *three* years correspond to Jesus' three years of ministry to the Jewish people, yet their leaders still refused to accept Him as the Messiah and the Son of God?

21 The rebirth of the nation of Israel was fulfilled on May 14, 1948. It became an independent state at about the time the leaves of fig trees start to emerge. Amazing!

in March or April. Consequently, this tree is certainly different than normal.[22]

If someone told me that the Lord made the tree to grow its leaves in March to represent the deceitful Israel, I would believe it. Why? In the Old Testament, the Lord God made a plant grow one day and made it wither the next:

> Then the LORD God provided a vine and made it grow up over Jonah to give shade for his head to ease his discomfort, and Jonah was very happy about the vine. But at dawn the next day God provided a worm, which chewed the vine so that it withered. (Jonah 4:6-7, NIV)

Why cannot the Son of God do the same in the New Testament? He fed five thousand people with five loaves and two fish. If He could multiply loaves and fish, He certainly could grow leaves on this tree in the month of March (or any month) for His purpose as well. (His purpose will be discussed later.)

From the above, my conclusion is this: God selected Israel as His chosen nation in the Old Testament, and it was symbolized

---

22 We see the omniscience attribute of the Lord Jesus in His knowing Nathanael's innermost thought when he was under a distant fig tree (John 1:43–51). The Lord also knew the personal life of the Samaritan woman at the Jacob's well. She was so impressed that she confessed, "Come, see a man, which told me all things that ever I did: is not this the Christ?" (John 4:29, KJV; see vv. 5–42). So it is impossible for me to think that the Lord did not know the tree was barren in Mark 11.

by the fig tree. It is quite possible that this particular fig tree was also chosen by the Lord Jesus on purpose. It is hard for me to believe that this episode in Mark 11 is an accidental encounter. It is my belief that the Lord's divine power of foretelling is involved. (This is contrary to Wayne Jackson's conclusion that "Jesus did not exercise the full range of his divine powers constantly; He did not know the details regarding this tree until He was in close proximity.")

A question will naturally arise: If the Lord already knew the tree was barren, why did He approach it? Good question. Let's examine that.

Utterly Faithful Jesus

Mark 11:13 continues, "He went to see if perhaps He would find *anything* on it" (emphasis added). My question is why the Scripture does not say, "He went to see if perhaps He would find *something* on it." However, rather than "something on it" the Scripture reads, "anything on it." Could it be that the Lord did not expect to find anything on it from the beginning? If so, the Lord did exercise His omniscience. But then what was the Lord doing? Let's dig deeper for hidden treasures.

The fig tree is the symbol of Israel, and if the Lord was to accuse Israel for their spiritual barrenness, He had to have two or more witnesses to attest to the fact that the fig tree was barren. The Scripture says, "You shall not bear false witness against your neighbor." (Deut. 5:20).

The Ten Commandments were given by God, and Jesus is one of the three Persons in the Trinity. Thus, the above command is also given by the Lord Jesus, namely, "One witness is not enough to convict a man accused of any crime or offense he may have committed. A matter must be established by the testimony of two or three witnesses" (Deut. 19:15, NIV). To be faithful to His own Word, He needed more than one witness before His accusation of Israel could be established.

Jesus said, "I did not come to abolish the Law of Moses or the writings of the prophets. No, I came to fulfill them." (see Matt. 5:17, NLT). The Lord is utterly humble and faithful. He abided by His own Law as an example for us to follow.

> Jesus said to them, "I tell you the truth, at the renewal of all things, when the Son of Man sits on his glorious throne, you who have followed me will also sit on twelve thrones, judging the twelve tribes of Israel." (Matt. 19:28, NIV)

This verse tells us why He needed twelve witnesses, not just two or three.

Finally, verse 14 reads, "He said to it, 'May no one ever eat fruit from you again!' And His disciples were listening." The last sentence is to confirm that the disciples heard and saw the act of the Lord. This emphasis had made them a group of *valid witnesses*, and the accusation was established. If it were not for the witnessing, this sentence would be redundant and serve no purpose, for if the disciples had not seen it and heard it, Mark would not have included this sentence in his narration. This sentence is important in the sense that it is equivalent to the wording such as, "The undersigned has read and understood" before a witness signs a present-day legal document. I believe the Scripture does not waste words, and every word has its purpose.

In concluding this section, I believe the Lord was *not* angry just because He could not find any fruit to eat. Rather He was establishing the evidence as the basis for His accusation. Could this be a long-ignored truth—a hidden treasure that Jesus is indeed an omniscient Lord here as well as in many other places in the Scripture?

The Bible says in John 1:10, "He was in the world, and though the world was made through Him, the world did not recognize Him" (NIV). Israel is a nation chosen by God. The Lord wanted the people of Israel to be the first nation to recognize Jesus as the Messiah and to have all the nations of the world come to know Him through them. But contrary to His wish, the chosen people did not accept Him; even worse, they crucified Him. Clearly it was not the season. In fact, it was not possible for the nation of Israel to bear fruit, so long as the Jewish leaders rejected Jesus as the Savior of humankind.

If the above interpretation is acceptable, we do not need to defend the Lord by giving lengthy explanations that the Lord was looking for "edible buds" when it was not the season for figs, as the other commentators do.

The Curse

The day, on which the Lord Jesus made the fig tree wither, was the day following His triumphal entry into Jerusalem riding on a colt. In three more days, those Jewish people who once shouted "Hosanna!" were going to shout, "Crucify Him!"

The Scripture says:

> When Pilate saw that he was getting nowhere, but that instead uproar was starting, he took water and washed his hands in front of the crowd. "I am innocent of this man's blood," he said. "It is your responsibility!"
>
> All the people answered, "Let his blood be on us and on our children!" (Matt. 27:24–25, NIV)

Clearly, the Lord Jesus' curse on the fig tree was, in fact, a *prophetic* statement that, in three days, the Jewish people were going to curse themselves and even their children and that the self-cursing would be fulfilled by the destruction of the nation of Israel, symbolized by the withering of the fig tree.

The treasure is that the Lord Jesus never did anything unreasonable. He is a merciful and compassionate Savior after all. If He meant to curse the Israel people, He would not have prayed for them on the cross, "Father, forgive them, for they do not know what they are doing." (Luke 23:34, NIV)

A critic, who believes that it was a curse by the Lord, and not a prophecy, maintains that cursing and forgiveness do not necessarily preclude each other; thus, he believes that the Lord Jesus can curse the nation of Israel and then ask the Father to forgive them on the cross. I cannot agree more if this critic has in mind that the Lord God in the Old Testament often cursed Israel and then promised to restore her. Perhaps the history of the Old Testament has made this critic conclude that cursing and forgiveness do not necessarily preclude each other. However, here in Mark 11, if the curse was not a curse by the Lord but a prophecy of self-cursing by the Jewish people, as I believe, then there is nothing to preclude, for there was no cursing but only forgiveness.

When the Lord Jesus prayed, "For they do not know what they are doing", the Lord was on the cross. Thus, I believe He was referring to the act of the Jewish leaders and the Roman soldiers who were crucifying Him.

I believe His prayer was referring to two facts: (1) they *did not know* the man they crucified was the Son of God; (2) the Jewish leaders wanted to crucify the Lord Jesus so badly that they even dared to curse themselves, and they *did not know* the seriousness of their self-cursing, which would eventually lead to the destruction of Israel.

I believe the passage of the fig tree, *together* with the cleansing of the temple, was a call to the Jewish people of that *generation* to repent or perish! The judgment will finally come, "When the Son of Man sits on his glorious throne, you who have followed me will also sit on twelve thrones, judging the twelve tribes of Israel." (Matt. 19:28, NIV)

The Teaching to the Twelve

I believe this passage about the fig tree is a prophecy that the Jewish people of that generation must repent or they would perish like that fig tree. At the same time, it is also foretelling what would happen to the twelve disciples. His twelve disciples would bear witness of Him as the Messiah, even when they were under persecution (not the season for figs). He predicted that their testimony (early buds) would eventually become the foundation of the early Christian church (the first harvest of figs). Again, what Jesus did was a prophecy as well as His plan for His disciples.

Cleansing the Temple

Some adult Sunday school students wonder why a paragraph on the cleansing of the temple is inserted between two parts of one event—that is, part 1: Jesus cursed the fig tree, part 2: the fig tree withered as a result, and in between is this act of temple cleansing. On the other hand, in Matthew 21:12–22, the cleansing of the temple preceded both the cursing and withering of the fig tree, as if the two events, cursing and cleansing, were completely independent.

I believe that Mark recorded the events chronologically, while Matthew recorded the events by grouping the Lord's teachings. As a result, Matthew's writing tends to make a reader focus on the teaching that the power of prayer can even cast a mountain into the sea, if and only if the person who prays does not have the slightest doubt in his or her heart.

However, according to the more chronological record of Mark, I cannot help but think that the cleansing of the temple was not an isolated event; it is closely related to the Lord's act on the fig tree, because of His choice to intertwine the two events. He could have cleansed the temple earlier, for it was not the only time He had visited the temple. Maybe the Lord did this cleansing here because He knew the time to go to Calvary was near. But then we can ask why He chose to place the cleansing after the cursing and before the withering of the fig tree.

I believe Jesus wanted the disciples to learn something more than the miracle of faith; He cleansed the temple because the people had turned the house of prayer into a den of robbers. Their greed could be compared to *inedible, bad figs* (see Jeremiah 24:8; 29:17). Thus, prophesying the future destruction of Israel (symbolized by the withered fig tree) and cleansing the temple (by rebuking the greedy people, symbolized by inedible bad figs) may in fact be one act.

While the first was intended *for the disciples* to be His witnesses and a prophecy for the disciples' future; the cleansing of the temple was intended *for the public*, calling them to repent lest they perish. By believing that every move the Lord made had a purpose, the Scripture would lead us to the treasure: Jesus is indeed the Son of God.

Further Reflection

Having said all this, I recall the encouragement that Paul gave to Timothy in his second letter. Second Timothy 4:2 says, "Preach the Word; be ready in season and out of season; reprove, rebuke, exhort, with great patience and instruction."

It is interesting to note the phrase "out of season" here and the phrase "not the season" in Mark 11. Could this verse be Paul's *application* of the Lord's teaching in Mark 11? He wanted the young Timothy to keep witnessing (early buds) for the Lord, even when he was under unfavorable circumstances (out of season—a young man among mature false teachers). As for Paul's admonition to "reprove, rebuke, exhort," it is strikingly similar to cleansing the temple. Remember that Paul did elsewhere compare our body to the temple.

Summary

- The consistency and integrity of the Bible: When readers do not fully understand a part of the Scripture, God provides the answers somewhere else in the Bible. Although there are sixty-six books, they are in fact one completely integrated Bible. I can understand why Pastor Rick Warren stresses that students *must* correlate their new insights or findings with the scriptures they know.

- The Bible is true yesterday, today, and forever. What the Lord Jesus taught His twelve disciples was valid in the days of Paul and is still valid today for today's church.

- The Lord Jesus is indeed the Son of God, who is omnipotent (making the fig tree wither), omniscient (prophesying the self-cursing of the Jews and its consequence—the destruction of the nation of Israel), and omnipresent (His Words still impact our lives today, even to eternity).

Application

- The Jewish people cursed themselves from their own mouths, and the destruction of Israel came to pass. Let's learn the wisdom from the Scripture: "Put away perversity from your mouth; keep corrupt talk far from your lips." (Prov. 4:24, NIV).

- In response to the Savior's teaching, we are charged to bear fruit, not to display ourselves as Christians and as a Christian church in outward appearances only. We are to trust the teaching of the Word and obey with our deeds.

It was September 1960 when I came to this country for the first time. The streets of the whole town of New Haven, Connecticut, were deserted on Sundays. What a beautiful sight, because all the stores were closed for business on Sundays and all the residents were in churches worshipping their Creator.

Today, atheists want the government to remove the phrase "In God We Trust" from U.S. currency, remove prayer from classrooms in public schools, and remove any structure related to religion from public buildings. Cassie Bernall, who answered "Yes" to the killer's question, "Do you believe in God?" was shot to death in the Columbine High School massacre (in which fifteen died and twenty-four were injured) in Colorado on April 20, 1999. It is unconceivable to me how this country, which used to be so godly and the most prosperous in the world, has become such an ungodly and deeply debt-ridden nation. I believe the only way to restore this country to its past greatness is to again become a God-fearing nation. For the Scripture says,

> The wicked return to the grave, all the nations
> that forget God. (Ps. 9:17, NIV)

The eyes of the LORD are on those who fear him,

on those whose hope is in his unfailing love. (Ps.

33:18, NIV)

3. Was the Prophecy Unfulfilled?
Jeremiah 22:18–19; 36:30; 2 Kings 24:6

———————— ✌ ————————

> Literary genre is crucial to interpretation ...
> Unless you know what types of literature
> those are taken from, you are in no position
> to determine their meaning!
>
> H. G. and W. D. Hendricks, *Living by the Book*,
> 209.

An academically oriented professor of theology invited bloggers to respond to his new finding in the Scripture on a Web site[23]. Maybe he was trying to stimulate bloggers' reflections. According to him, he has found that the inspired prophecies in the Old Testament are not always fulfilled, at least not in the exact way they were originally prophesied. This professor compared the prophecies in the book of Jeremiah with the outcome in 2 Kings as follows,

---

23 http://www.answertheskeptic.com/index.php/unfulfilled-prophesies/2008/12/11

Therefore this is what the LORD says about Jehoiakim son of Josiah, king of Judah:

"They will not mourn for him:

'Alas, my brother! Alas, my sister!'

They will not mourn for him:

'Alas, my master! Alas, his splendor!'

He will have the burial of a donkey—dragged away and thrown outside the gates of Jerusalem."

(Jere. 22:18-19, NIV)

Therefore, this is what the LORD says about Jehoiakim king of Judah: He will have no one to sit on the throne of David; his body will be thrown out and exposed to the heat by day and the frost by night. (Jere. 36:30, NIV)

The professor says that the above prophecies were not fulfilled, because the outcome ended up:

Jehoiakim rested with his fathers. And Jehoiachin his son succeeded him as king. (2 Kings 24:6, NIV)

He concludes that 2 Kings 24:6 shows that Jeremiah's prophecies failed.

Literary Genres and Interpretation

While the Book of Jeremiah is a book of prophecies, the books of Kings and Chronicles are history books. The literary expression of prophets is different from that of historians, and their sources also differ. Prophets convey God's messages through divine inspiration, and historians write from human sources. Jeremiah died in Egypt; thus the author of 2 Kings is believed to be someone who came back later from captivity. The resources for the author of the history are believed to be from the annals of the kings of Israel and the kings of Judah in the palaces (see 2 Kings 24:5; 2 Chron. 36:8). The historians record history by straightforward narratives, while prophets often convey God's message in metaphors, similes, other figures of speech, or direct words.

Prophets Conveying God's Messages

While the Bible says, "Jehoiakim rested with his fathers," the Web site says, "Jehoiakim received a proper burial." The words "rested with his fathers" simply mean he died, which is a common expression in the Bible, and there is no indication that it means "he received a *proper* burial." The word *proper* is added by the professor. Jehoiakim died. That is a fact, thus the history book recorded it in straight narratives as "he rested with his fathers," for they do not use the word "died."

However, Jeremiah is a prophet, and how a prophet conveys the Lord's will is a unique literary genre in the Bible. For example, in Isaiah 66:1, the Scripture says, "Thus says the LORD, 'Heaven is My throne and the earth is My footstool.'" This is a metaphoric expression, using the greatest wording that Isaiah could to exalt the Almighty. The true meaning behind this is that the *greatness* of the Lord is beyond human comprehension.

Here in the Book of Jeremiah, the prophet was using simile (*like* the burial of a donkey) to convey God's message. The bottom line is that the prophet was describing how *angry* the Lord God was about Jehoiakim, for he refused to listen to Him and misguided His people to sin.

As for Jeremiah's prophecy, "They will not mourn for him: 'Alas, my *brother*! Alas, my *sister*!'"(emphasis added) means that even a commoner's death, male or female, is mourned by his or her families or relatives, but no family members or relatives will lament for Jehoiakim in his dishonorable death.

And "They will not mourn for him: 'Alas, my master! Alas, his splendor!'" means that his servants will not mourn for him as their *master*, and the people of his kingdom will not mourn for him as their *king*. It is just a description of a very pitiful death.

I once heard an anecdote about a college student who complained to his professor about the grade he got, saying, "I think I do not deserve to get an F in your class," and the professor *agreed*: "I think you do not deserve to get an F too, but unfortunately, in this school I can give students no grade lower than F." The point is that if Jeremiah had known any other wording that could downgrade even more the worthlessness of Jehoiakim's life and death, he would have used it to convey the *anger* of God about this wicked king. Thus Jeremiah used simile to compare Jehoiakim's death with a donkey's death.

In 2 Chronicles, the Scripture says: "Nebuchadnezzar king of Babylon came up against him [Jehoiakim] and bound him with bronze chains to take him to Babylon." (36:6)

This verse suggests that he was taken outside the gate of Jerusalem and died there, or he might have died in the desert on his way to Babylon. Jeremiah 36:30 says that his body would be thrown out and exposed to the heat by day and the frost by night. Clearly, the prophecies of Jeremiah were fulfilled.

The Successor to the King's Throne

The prophecy says, "Therefore, this is what the Lord says about Jehoiakim king of Judah: He will have no one to sit on the throne of David" (Jere. 36:30, NIV). On the other hand the history book says, "Jehoiachin his son succeeded him as king" (2 Kings 24:6). The professor quoted this verse to support his finding that the prophecy failed. Again the importance of literary genres in interpretation is revealed here.

Second Kings 24:6 records the fact that Jehoiachin succeeded his father Jehoiakim as a king. It is a historical fact and should be recorded as such in the history book, the annals of the kings of Judah.

However, when the Lord says through Jeremiah that none of Jehoiakim's offspring will sit on the throne of David, I believe that the Lord God is referring to the fact that Jehoiachin was never anointed to become a king by a God-appointed prophet or judge as David was by Samuel. The Scripture specifically stressed "the throne of David", and I believe the mention of David must have special meaning in the interpretation of prophecy.

It also shows that the Scripture never wastes words. Jehoiachin succeeded his father Jehoiakim as the king of Judah for three months and was taken prisoner to Babylon by Nebuchadnezzar. In fact the last four kings of Judah—Jehoahaz, Jehoiakim, Jehoiachin, and Zedekiah—were never anointed by God as King David was. They were vassal kings of foreign powers, either Egypt or Babylon. The words "the throne" represent authority and power that none of these wicked kings were given by the almighty God. In conclusion, I believe the prophecies of Jeremiah by inspiration of God were fulfilled.

Summary

- History books record events from human perspective, while the prophecy books disclose God's will from His perspective.

- History books use narrative to describe historical events, while prophecy books often use metaphors, similes, or symbols. The "How-to" books remind us to be careful that the literary genres of the passages call for proper interpretation.

Application

Let us live a life such as Paul taught in Colossians 1:10 (NIV): "And we pray this in order that you may live a life worthy of the Lord and may please him in every way: bearing fruit in every good work, growing in the knowledge of God ..."

4. The Earth Is His Footstool
Isaiah 66:1–2

—————————— ❧ ——————————

Interpret the Scripture in the figurative sense if a literal meaning is impossible or absurd. Yet He expects us to read them as symbols, not absurdities.

H. G. and W. D. Hendricks, *Living By the Book*, 261.

With the advent of the Internet, there are many Web sites related to the Christian faith. Some can help the spiritual growth of their readers. But some bloggers' questions and discussions can also confuse believers. Let us select a case for our meditation. In this chapter we will reflect on interpretation of metaphors.[24]

An adult Sunday school teacher in our church called my attention to a skeptic's question about the consistency of the

---

24 Hendricks and Hendricks, *Living by the Book*, 257.

Bible. The two Bible passages that the skeptic quoted are as in the following:[25]

> The LORD appeared to him (King Solomon) at night and said: "I have heard your prayer and have chosen this place for myself as a temple for sacrifices ... I have chosen and consecrated this temple so that my Name may be there forever. My eyes and my heart will always be there." (2 Chron. 7:12, 16, NIV)

And another verse,

> However, the Most High does not live in houses made by men. (Acts 7:48, NIV)

He wrongly concluded the 2 Chronicles passage says, "God dwells in temples," but Stephen's speech in the book of Acts says, "God dwells *not* in temples." The skeptic thought that the two passages were contradicting each other.

The Omnipresence of God

The fact is that both the aforementioned scriptures never said that God dwelled in the temple built by Solomon. I think

---

25 The question by the skeptic was in the website http://www.answertheskeptic.com/index.php/bible-difficulty/2008/08/08

this misinterpretation stems from the misunderstanding of the statement in 2 Chronicles 7:16, "My eyes and my heart will always be there." The questioner is trying to understand God by applying categories of the human physical body. The eyes and heart are parts of our physical body, and where our eyes and heart are, our entire body has to be there.

However, Jesus said, "God is spirit, and those who worship Him must worship in spirit and truth (John 4:24)." Thus God is an omnipresent Spirit, He is everywhere, and He does not dwell in man-made houses. He knows and sees anything and everything, without the need of eyes and heart in human flesh.

Another possibility is that the skeptic's misinterpretation of the passage could have stemmed from the human concept of a dwelling place. From man's perspective, a dwelling place is defined by a space surrounded by walls. The truth is that God existed before He created space and time. Thus, there is no human concept of space and walls to Him! In other words, space and time cannot confine or limit God, as they do people.

David described the omnipresence of God in the Book of Psalms:

> Where can I go from your Spirit?
>
> Where can I flee from your presence?
>
> If I go up to the heavens, you are there;
>
> if I make my bed in the depths, you are there.

If I rise on the wings of the dawn,

if I settle on the far side of the sea,

Even there your hand will guide me;

your right hand will hold me fast. (Ps. 139:7–10, NIV)

The point is that we should not attempt to measure the infinite God with our limited understanding, just as the Bible tells us: "Trust in the LORD with all your heart and lean not on your own understanding" (Prov. 3:5, NIV).

We should be glad that He is omnipresent. No matter where we are and whether we are in sickness, in financial difficulties, in the loss of loved ones, or in time of distress, we are assured of His presence and His help—His hand will guide us and His right hand will hold us fast, as David put it in the Psalm just quoted.

Contrary to what the skeptic thinks, we can see that 2 Chronicles 7:12 says God *does not* dwell in a man-made temple:

- It says that the Lord God heard Solomon's prayer, when the temple was completed. Clearly, God had already had His place, even before Solomon started building one.

- God said "I have chosen this place as a temple of sacrifice." He did not say, "A place of My dwelling."

- The Lord Jesus said "In My Father's house are many dwelling places; if it were not so, I would have told you; for I go to prepare a place for you." (John 14:2) The Lord Jesus certainly cannot be referring to the temple built by King Solomon.

God has chosen to accept the man-made temple as a house of sacrifice (v. 12) and as a house of prayer (v. 15) and has promised that He will hear our prayers from heaven (vv. 14–15). Not that God needs a man-made place, but He *designated* the temple as a place for our worship, prayer, and offering, merely to *accommodate* the limitation of humankind.

The Focus of the Passages

One of the keys to meditation is to constantly ask, "What is the Scripture trying to teach us? In a given passage, what should we place our focus on?" The most important part of this passage is, in fact, in verses 14 and 15; but somehow the skeptic omitted them entirely in his question on the Web site. This is one example of taking the text (v. 16) out of context (vv. 14–15). The verses that the blogger omitted are shown below:

> If my people, who are called by my name, will humble themselves and pray and seek my face and turn from their wicked ways, then will I hear from heaven and will forgive their sin and will

heal their land. Now my eyes will be open and my ears attentive to the prayers offered in this place. (2 Chron. 7:14–15, NIV)

Verses 15 and 16 mean that the Lord promises to watch over the people of Israel, to listen to their prayers, and to accept their offerings in His *designated* temple. The sentence, "will I hear from heaven" means "You pray down there, and I hear your prayers up here." This should make it sufficiently clear that the Lord God is not confined by anybody, anywhere.

In this case of 2 Chronicles, the teaching is this: God would grant His promises, only if people would "humble themselves," "pray and seek the Lord God," and "turn away from wickedness" (v. 14). These requirements should be the focus of the passages in question, not whether God can or cannot dwell in temples.

As for Acts 7:48, which the blogger quoted, its focus should be in its context that Stephen quoted from the book of Isaiah, namely,

Thus says the LORD,

"Heaven is My throne and the earth is My footstool.

Where then is a house you could build for Me?

And where is a place that I may rest?

For My hand made all these things,

Thus all these things came into being," declares the LORD.

"But to this one I will look,

To him who is humble and contrite of spirit, and

who trembles at My word." (Isaiah 66:1–2)

This is quoted by Stephen in Acts 7:49–50. The Lord is saying that the pagan gods are human creations, and people place them in houses built for them. But the Lord God is Creator of the universe and everything in it. Men would never be able to build a structure large enough for God's house, because the largest house that men could possibly build would be at most as large as the planet Earth itself, and the Lord God is saying that planet Earth is only a small part in His creation (*metaphorically* as small as His footstool). The truth behind the metaphor is that His greatness and omnipotent attributes are beyond human comprehension. The lesson is that the truth behind the metaphor is greater than the literal description itself.

Verse 2 is saying that, however small and insignificant man's physical existence is in God's creation (Ps. 8:3–4), He promises to look after those people with love and compassion, who are God-fearing and humble to confess their sins, those who respect, trust, and obey His Word.

Again, this focal point quoted by Stephen in Acts is exactly the same as the focal point in 2 Chronicles 7:14–15. There is no contradiction at all. On the contrary, the Scripture is consistent in all sixty-six books.

Why Does the Bible Use Metaphor?

Our thoughts and ways are so limited that we would never be able to know God unless He reveals Himself to us. However, He reveals only to the extent that humans can express their limited understanding of Him. To Isaiah, the earth that he stood on and the heaven that he gazed upon were the biggest things he had ever known. Thus, he could only use the greatest things that he could imagine to poetically express the greatness of God.

However, we know now that the earth is only a small planet in the solar system, and the sun is only a small star in the Milky Way galaxy, which has more than 700 million stars; and the Milky Way galaxy is only one of the countless billions of galaxies in the universe.

If Isaiah had known all these facts in his time, he would probably have expressed his praise of God differently, because he had underestimated the size of God's foot (metaphorically) or overestimated the size of the earth in the universe.

In view of all this, should we revise the Scripture by saying that the entire universe, instead of just the earth, is the footstool of God? If we have to revise the Scripture, the Bible wouldn't be infallible, for it would be time-variant.

But the fact is even if we say that the whole universe, instead of the earth, is *metaphorically* the footstool of the Almighty, we would still be confining God in a small space that our limited thoughts and ways can imagine. The truth is that we do not even know how large the universe is. How can we imagine the greatness of its Creator?

The Lord God is revealing His greatness and omnipresence metaphorically. The absolute truth behind the metaphor never changes in time, no matter how human knowledge progresses. As human knowledge progresses, the Holy Spirit will be ready to teach us *more* from the *same* metaphor; thus no revision is required. This is further proof that the Scripture is God-breathed with His wisdom.

Attitude for Meditation

There is nothing wrong about seekers, believers, or even skeptics asking questions. On the contrary, the key to a fruitful meditation is to ask as many questions as one possibly can (Ref: Hendricks and Hendricks). It is the teaching of the Holy Spirit through our meditation that leads to an accurate interpretation of His will.

It is the mental attitude of the asking individual that can cause problems. If questions are motivated by earnestly seeking the truth to help one's faith, then I believe the Holy Spirit will teach and guide us. However, if a question is prompted by creating issues to argue about the Scripture, it would only harden skeptical hearts and confirm their blindness to the truth.

Summary

- The Bible often uses figurative speech in the form of allegories, symbols, similes, metaphors, and parables. The hidden treasure is the truth behind the figurative speech.

- The truth behind the figurative expression is greater than the literal meaning itself and is time invariant, no matter how human civilization or understanding progresses.

- Meditation on the spiritual meaning behind the literal description of Scripture would enhance the joy of Bible reading, provided that our reflection conforms to the teaching of the Bible (Ref: Hendricks and Hendricks, page 28).

- Let us seek the truth with humble and sincere attitude, with the desire to walk closer to our Creator through His Son Jesus Christ.

- Almost all promises in the Scripture are conditional. The Lord God will honor His promises only when we humble ourselves, pray and seek His face, and turn from our wicked ways.

Application

Because the Lord God is omnipresent, we can praise and give thanks to Him anywhere, in our going out, in our coming in, and in our lying down (see Ps. 121:8; 139:2–3; Deut. 28:6; 1 Thess. 5:16–18). When you find a parking spot near the entrance to a supermarket, thank the Lord for the convenience. When you find a parking spot far from the entrance, thank Him for the opportunity to do exercise walking for a distance.

Have you ever experienced getting impatient and annoyed by waiting in a car for the red traffic light to turn green, especially when you are in a hurry to catch a train, an airplane, or a doctor's appointment? Try this: clap your hands and keep reciting loudly, "Rejoice always; pray without ceasing; in everything give thanks." (1 Thess. 5:16–18) Most important, *believe* that "this is God's will for you in Christ Jesus" (v. 18).

You should experience the following results:

1. The feeling of irritation and annoyance at waiting for the red light will disappear into thin air. This is important for your mental health.

2. By clapping your hands, you can improve the blood circulation to your fingertips. This is important for your physical health.

3. By reciting the Scripture out loud, you can concentrate on its meaning and enhance your faith. This is important for your spiritual health.

Most important, the omnipresent Lord is listening, and He knows your heart, no matter where you are, for the Scripture says,

> You know when I sit and when I rise;
>
> you perceive my thoughts from afar.
>
> You discern my going out and my lying down;
>
> you are familiar with all my ways.
>
> Before a word is on my tongue
>
> you know it completely, O LORD. (Ps. 139:2–4, NIV)

On the other hand, the omnipresent attribute of God is negatively applied by certain people. I have seen cases when a church needs to build or expand facilities for ministries, and some members of the congregation are bound to object. The reasons vary; a frequent one is that fund raising will drive members away from the church. The most off-beat argument is that God does not dwell in a temple or church anyway, as the Bible says, so why go to such expense for constructing a center for worship, education, or fellowship?

The same argument that "God does not dwell in a man-made building" leads some people to stop going to local church and have their Sunday services at home by listening to sermons on television. Fortunately, most of the TV-evangelical preachers urge the home viewers to join a local church, which is *faithfully teaching* the Bible. Not that God needs a man-made place, but He designated a temple or a church as a place for our worship, prayer, and offering, merely to *accommodate* our limited thoughts and ways. Thus we should join a church and never cease to congregate with the brothers and sisters in Christ for spiritual growth (see Heb. 10:24–25).

5. A Slave Girl, a Military Commander, and a Man of God

2 Kings 5:1–27

Identifying Character Qualities

> Identify character qualities taught in the Bible with the view of learning to avoid the negative ones and learning to work on the positive ones, so that we become more like the Lord Jesus Christ.
>
> Rick Warren, *Bible Study Methods*, 62.

"Faith by itself, if it is not accompanied by action, is dead" (James 2:17, NIV). In the same way, Bible study without application to daily life is like learning to play a piano by just reading books about the musical instrument. Thus, the application of Scripture is one of the three essentials—namely observation, interpretation, and application—which are taught by each and every book on how to study the Bible.

In 2 Kings 5, there are many characters from which we can learn to better ourselves as Christians.[26] Let us reflect on this passage for verse-by-verse application, as we identify the qualities of these characters.

In the NIV version, the Scripture says,

> [1] Now Naaman was commander of the army of the king of Aram. He was a great man in the sight of his master and highly regarded, because through him the Lord had given victory to Aram. He was a valiant soldier, but he had leprosy.
>
> [2] Now bands from Aram had gone out and had taken captive a young girl from Israel, and she served Naaman's wife. [3] She said to her mistress, "If only my master would see the prophet who is in Samaria! He would cure him of his leprosy."

Verse 1 introduces the man Naaman as a military commander, who is a great man in the sight of his master, the king of Aram, because he has won many battles for his king[27]. In verses 2–3, we can identify positive qualities of a nameless young maidservant

---

26 An excellent verse-by-verse interpretation of this chapter has been given by John F. Walvoord and Roy B. Zuck, *The Bible Knowledge Commentary O.T.* (Vector Books, 1984)

27 In this chapter, "Historical Present" is extensively used, instead of using past tense.

from Israel, who I believe is a great girl in the sight of God, because she helps win the soul of Naaman for the Lord.

Although Naaman might not be directly involved, the soldiers of Aram, often enemies of Israel, have taken this girl captive. She was forced to leave her home, her family, and her people at a young age. She was once free in Israel, but has been captured to live in a foreign country against her will and probably sold to become a slave to serve Naaman's wife. Though being a captive, she has sympathy and compassion for her captors' military commander, her mistress's husband, who has leprosy.

The Slave Girl's Positive Quality

Undoubtedly, this girl had the God-given gift of loving her enemy and a spirit of absolute faith in God.

She lived in the era of the two kingdoms after Solomon, Israel in the north and Judea in the south, when she only heard the traditional practice of "eye for eye, tooth for tooth" (Exod. 21:23–25) and at best, "love your neighbor as yourself" (Levit. 19:18)—but not "love your enemy," which comes only from the teaching of the Lord Jesus (Matt. 5:44). Perhaps Naaman and his wife were kind to this maidservant, and she wanted to reciprocate. Therefore, her motive may not have been "love your enemy" in the strict sense as the Lord Jesus teaches, but she certainly had the positive quality of "loving the unlovable."

I believe we all have experienced that it is easier said than done to love our enemies. Yet the Bible is teaching us to learn to be more like Jesus. May the Holy Spirit mold and change us, possibly in four steps as we (1) forgive but cannot forget, (2) forgive and forget, (3) love the unlovable, and finally (4) love our enemy. The Lord Jesus preached and practiced step four. Even though loving our enemy may become easier in light of Paul's recognition that "our struggle is not against flesh and blood" (Ephesians 6:12; see verses 10–18), we must admit that without the example of the Lord Jesus and the help of the Holy Spirit, we cannot even reach the second step.

The Hebrew slave girl had an absolute faith in God and His prophet. Her positive qualities were these: (1) She never thought for a moment about the "what ifs"—*what if* the prophet failed to heal her master, and her recommendation caused her master to travel so far to Samaria in vain? *What if* her master turned his frustration on her as a result and made her life miserable from then on? Naaman's leprosy was incurable. If it could have been cured, he, in his powerful and wealthy position, would have had someone heal him of his disease long before. The slave girl's courage to make a suggestion to her master must have stemmed from her absolute faith in God and His prophet.

(2) She had the zeal and passion for evangelism to share her faith with a Gentile. How often do we feel reluctant to talk about our faith, for fear of being ridiculed by skeptics or even our friends? How often do we forget that we are tools of the Holy Spirit, who is the One moving in us to win souls; just as gloves are only tools to a surgeon, who is the one moving his hands in

the gloves to mend a patient's flesh? This nameless slave maid definitely teaches lessons for us to learn: (a) Share Jesus with people around us, and (b) believe that the Holy Spirit will work in a mysterious way. Even the Lord Jesus said, "No one can come to me unless the Father who sent me draws him, and I will raise him up at the last day" (John 6:44, NIV).

King Ben-Hadad of Aram

The Scripture continues,

> [4] Naaman went to his master and told him what the girl from Israel had said. [5] "By all means, go," the king of Aram replied. "I will send a letter to the king of Israel." So Naaman left, taking with him ten talents of silver, six thousand shekels of gold and ten sets of clothing. [6] The letter that he took to the king of Israel read: "With this letter I am sending my servant Naaman to you so that you may cure him of his leprosy."

Verses 4 and 6 confirm the statement of verse 1 that Naaman was a favorite military commander of the king of Aram. He not only accepted Naaman's sick leave from his duty, but also kindly volunteered to write a letter for him to bring along, hoping that it would help Naaman gain favor in the sight of the king of Israel. This kind gesture of the king of Aram is an example of leading subordinates by kindness and not by fear. However, the king's act is only a normal human reaction, for Naaman was loyal and invaluable to him. In contrast to this, the Lord Jesus is commanding His followers to reach an even higher level of love and kindness. The Lord Jesus says,

> If you love those who love you, what reward will you get? Are not even the tax collectors doing that? And if you greet only your brothers, what are you doing more than others? Do not even pagans do that? Be perfect, therefore, as your heavenly Father is perfect. (Matt. 5:46–48, NIV)

We recognize three facts: (1) Jesus shows us how imperfect we are, for we only love those who love us. (2) The Lord Jesus did not just preach and demand that we change; He preached it and demonstrated it Himself for our example, for He prayed to the Father to forgive those who crucified Him. Finally, (3) God the Father is perfect, and with the help of the Holy Spirit, the Lord Jesus wants us to change ourselves to be *more* like Him, who is also perfect, so that we can walk with Him day by day and become acceptable to the Father at eternity.

The first fact prompts us to be humble and calls for our confession of faith in Him. The second fact calls for change in our character, even if it takes lifelong learning and practice. The third fact calls for knowing our purpose in life: to be more like

Jesus and influence others, even if it may mean that we can only make progress in small steps one day at a time.

King Joram of Israel

> [7] As soon as the king of Israel read the letter, he tore his robes and said, "Am I God? Can I kill and bring back to life? Why does this fellow send someone to me to be cured of his leprosy? See how he is trying to pick a quarrel with me!"

Here we can see two negative qualities of the king of Israel which we should learn to avoid: (1) When the king of Israel read the letter, the first thing that came to his mind was not to seek the will of God but rather to suspect the intention of the king of Aram. Shouldn't he examine the situation first before jumping to conclusions? After all, Naaman had brought many valuable gifts with him—gold, silver, and clothing. If the king had asked Naaman how he came to the conclusion that Israel could heal him, he could have sensed the sincere intention of the commander.

Let us learn not to jump to conclusions in haste, for the Bible says, "My dear brothers, take note of this: Everyone should be quick to listen, slow to speak and slow to become angry" (James 1:19, NIV). It also implies that one should be slow to push the panic button before the facts are clear. Could this be a lesson for us and for world leaders especially, so as to avoid nuclear war in today's world?

(2) Unlike the nameless maidservant, the king of Israel did not have faith in God and His prophet. Church leaders should keep in mind that very often God gives us invaluable lessons through the least noticed members in our churches.

The Man of God vs. the Military Commander

> [8] When Elisha the man of God heard that the king of Israel had torn his robes, he sent him this message: "Why have you torn your robes? Have the man come to me and he will know that there is a prophet in Israel." [9] So Naaman went with his horses and chariots and stopped at the door of Elisha's house. [10] Elisha sent a messenger to say to him, "Go, wash yourself seven times in the Jordan, and your flesh will be restored and you will be cleansed."

Elisha, the man of God, came to rescue King Joram of his anxiety. He probably wanted Naaman, who was a Gentile, and the king of Israel, who had little faith, both to learn that there was a true prophet in Israel. Thus, when Naaman came to the door of Elisha's house with his men, his horses and chariots, and all the gifts, the prophet did not come out to receive him in person. Instead, he sent a messenger to tell this great military general to go skinny-dipping in the River Jordan seven times.

> [11] But Naaman went away angry and said, "I thought that he would surely come out to me and stand and call on the name of the LORD his God, wave his hand over the spot and cure me of my leprosy. [12] Are not Abana and Pharpar, the rivers of Damascus, better than any of the waters of Israel? Couldn't I wash in them and be cleansed?" So he turned and went off in a rage.

General Naaman got angry and went off in a rage. Walvoord and Zuck give the following two reasons: (1) His pride had been offended by Elisha's offhanded treatment of him. He had expected a cleansing ceremony in keeping with his own dignity. (2) He resented having been told to wash in a muddy river that he considered inferior to the rivers in his hometown. The water of Jordan, he thought, could not possibly do him any good.

Here, we can identify character defects revealed in the general Naaman. The Scripture constantly teaches us to be humble before God. It says, "You [God] save the humble but bring low those whose eyes are haughty" (Ps. 18:27, NIV). Also, "The eyes of the arrogant man will be humbled and the pride of men brought low" (Isaiah 2:11, NIV). By contrast, I believe that the Lord could discern Naaman's haughtiness and had Elisha treat the general offhandedly to see how he would respond. To the general, leprosy was a life or death affliction, and he felt ignored by an insolent prophet.

The prophet, on the other hand, took it as lightly as a mother telling a babysitter to put a band-aid on her child's scraped elbow. The Lord had shown His sense of humor, and Naaman got his firsthand lesson on humility. The healing power came from the Lord God. The prophet Elisha was just empowered by Him to see the general cured. Thus, obeying Elisha's instruction would mean obeying the Almighty.

What the Lord demanded of Naaman was to be humble and simply trust and obey. I believe the Lord God wanted Naaman to learn that it was neither a cleansing ceremony nor the water that cured his leprosy; it was the power of the Lord that healed him. If the Lord had told Naaman to dip in a river that was better than the rivers of Damascus, and he was cured as a result, he would have attributed his healing to the quality of the water and not the power of God. (In the same way, the Lord God gave Abraham and Sarah their son Isaac when Abraham was a hundred years old. He did not give Isaac to them when Abraham was thirty, lest he boast in their reproductive abilities and ignore God's blessing.)

How often do we pray to the Lord for healing, and after having been healed, we glorify the medical doctors or the drug manufacturers and forget about our prayers and God's healing power altogether? Granted, we do appreciate the contribution of medical doctors and pharmaceutical researchers, but a doctor is not God, he can make mistakes in judgment and use wrong medication, improper dosage, etc. As a doctor friend of mine puts it, "God heals the sick, and we doctors collect the rewards"; he is referring to the God-given self-healing immune systems in our body. Let us remember the teaching, "Be joyful always; pray continually; *give thanks* in all circumstances, for this is God's will for you in Christ Jesus" (1 Thess. 5:16–18, emphasis added).

The Scripture continues:

> [13] Naaman's servants went to him and said, "My father, if the prophet had told you to do some great thing, would you not have done it? How much more, then, when he tells you, 'Wash and be cleansed'!" [14] So he went down and dipped himself in the Jordan seven times, as the man of God had told him, and his flesh was restored and became clean like that of a young boy.

Verse 13 tells us that the nameless servants who accompanied Naaman to Samaria humbly advised their master to follow the Prophet Elisha's instruction. They essentially told Naaman that he would have nothing to lose but his disease of leprosy by trying to obey.

The Scripture says, "Listen to advice and accept instruction, and in the end you will be wise" (Prov. 19:20, NIV). General Naaman might be skillful in strategic planning at the battlefields, but his anger here kept him from thinking straight. The Scripture also says, "A fool gives full vent to his anger, but a wise man keeps himself under control" (Prov. 29:11, NIV). Lucky for Naaman, he was wise enough to control himself and listen to the advice that came from his lowly servants. He calmed down, humbly followed Elisha's instructions, and dipped himself in the River Jordan seven times. Miraculously, his dreadful leprosy was cured.

There are two lessons that we can learn from this story: (1) We should listen to advice based on its known truth, not based on the social status of the person giving the advice or the way in which they offer the advice. (2) Naaman listened to his servants' advice. Was it because the advice made sense to him, or was he so desperate to get rid of the dreadful disease that he felt he had no choice but to take the advice? We do not know. But there is one thing we do know: Because of his humble obedience to the Lord's instruction, not only was his body cleansed, but his eyes and heart were also opened to know the true God. Because the next verses say,

> 15 Then Naaman and all his attendants went back to the man of God. He stood before him and said, "Now I know that there is no God in all the

world except in Israel. Please accept now a gift
from your servant."

¹⁶ The prophet answered, "As surely as the LORD lives, whom I serve, I will not accept a thing." And even though Naaman urged him, he refused.

I believe that Naaman's comment, "Now I know that there is no God in all the world except in Israel" is the most beautiful confession of faith by a Gentile. From this resulting confession, we can understand the statement in verse 1 that says, "Because through him [Naaman] the LORD had given victory to Aram." The nation of Aram was the enemy of Israel, and yet why did the Lord give Naaman victory? I believe he was in the Lord's favor, for the omniscient God knew the general would eventually be converted and that, as a result, His name would be glorified. From this we recall what the Lord Jesus said when He restored the eyesight of a man who was *born* blind:

> As he [Jesus] went along, he saw a man blind
> from birth. His disciples asked him, "Rabbi, who
> sinned, this man or his parents, that he was
> born blind?"

"Neither this man nor his parents sinned," said Jesus, "but this happened so that the work of God might be displayed in his life." (John 9:1–3, NIV)

Could it be the same for Naaman, in that his suffering of leprosy happened so that the work of God might be displayed in his life? I believe so.

From this paragraph, two lessons can be added to our life applications: (1) The misfortunes that we encounter in our lives may turn into opportunities to display God's work in us, and our testimony of His mercy, compassion, and power can help seekers know there is a true God. (2) The man of God, Elisha, refused to receive any gifts from Naaman. I believe the Lord God, through His prophet, is telling us that *grace* is to be bestowed and cannot be purchased with earthly wealth. The way to acknowledge the grace of Jesus Christ is to listen to Him and to obey His teaching. For Christ says in the Scripture: "If anyone loves me, he will obey my teaching. My Father will love him, and we will come to him and make our home with him." (See John 14:23, NIV).

The Wicked Servant

Finally the chapter ends with the ungodly behavior of Gehazi, the servant of Elisha (2 Kings 5:19–26). After Naaman left Elisha, Gehazi ran after him and took two talents of silver and two sets of clothing from him. Several negative qualities are displayed here: (1) Gehazi's *greed* made him betray his master. While

Elisha swore in God's name not to take any gift from Naaman, Gehazi received a gift from Naaman for himself behind Elisha's back. (2) He *lied* that his action was his master's wish. Finally, (3) his *disobedience* to Elisha was in fact his disobedience to the Lord God. By his greed, the meaning of the "grace of God" was compromised. The negative qualities of Gehazi's character are certainly something we must work to avoid.

6. Science Is a Gift of God: (I)
—Creation Genesis 1:1–5

Gravity explains the motions of planets, but cannot explain who set the planets in motion. God governs all things and knows all that is or can be done.

—Isaac Newton

My religion consists of a humble admiration of the illimitable superior spirit who reveals himself in the slight details we are able to perceive with our frail and feeble mind.

Science without religion is lame. Religion without science is blind.[28]

—Albert Einstein

28 This author is aware that Einstein, fifteen months before his death, supposedly said in a private letter that he did not believe in a personal god. Since Stephen Hawking recently said the same, we discuss this subject in the last chapter of this book. See chapter 10 "Science and Religion Will Converge into Faith in God."

Being located in the heart of Silicon Valley, California, our church with a congregation of some 300 people has more than eighty individuals who have Ph.D.s in science and engineering. Some seekers among them confessed that they believe in the great teachings of Jesus,[29] but it is very difficult for them to believe in the six-day creation of the universe in the book of Genesis. The purpose of this chapter is to share my humble perception on this subject with my fellow engineers as well as seekers in general.

I quoted the saying of the aforementioned two great scientists, Isaac Newton and Albert Einstein, in order to remind myself that they believed in an illimitable superior spirit, whom we call God. If even these giants in science believe in the existence of God, who am I, a man with a feeble mind and limited knowledge of science, not to acknowledge the Creator of the universe?

Unlike Newton and Einstein, there are still many people who have some scientific knowledge but cannot humble themselves to accept God. Yet God loves these people regardless and has given humankind a quantum jump in scientific knowledge to know Him better, as prophesied in Daniel 12:4 (KJV), "But thou, O Daniel, shut up the words, and seal the book, even to the time of the end: many shall run to and fro, and knowledge shall be increased." I believe it was a promise as well as a prophecy. Daniel was told to shut up the words and seal the book until the end time. Now that God has given humanity remarkable knowledge and means of transportation and

---

29 Christians believe in Jesus, the Man who is God incarnated, not just His teachings. His teachings are to be trusted and practiced.

communication, we ought to be alert that the end time is near and prepare ourselves by humbly accepting Him. Considering that the promise was made at the time when people traveled on foot, the prophecy is plausibly fulfilled in our generation.

Let me illustrate how scientific and engineering knowledge are applied in sermons from church pulpits, so as to prove the point that religion and science do not have to be mutually exclusive. There are so many parallels and similarities in the two that having the knowledge of one can help us perceive the other.

In his Sunday sermon, Adrian Rogers[30] used the term *photosynthesis* to explain one of the reasons why the Lord Jesus said of Himself, "I am the Light of the world" (John 8:12) and "I am the bread of life" (John 6:35, 48). One type of photosynthesis commonly known to our daily life is a chemical process taking place in the leaves of plants, where light energy from the sun converts water from the roots and carbon dioxide from the air into sugar and oxygen molecules.[31] The sugar so produced is stored in fruits, vegetables, or roots, and the oxygen is released into the air. Both are *vital* to sustaining the life of organisms. Thus, aside from spiritual significance, scientific knowledge *enhances* our

---

30 The pastor and preacher of Bellevue Baptist Church and the "Love Worth Finding" TV ministry, Memphis, TN.

31 $6H_2O + 6CO_2 +$ Light Energy $=> C_6H_{12}O_6 + 6O_2$ (6 water and 6 carbon dioxide molecules converted into one sugar and 6 oxygen molecules by energy from sunlight). To Christians this is nothing new: in the Bible is found God's similar rule that He used to create man: Dust + His Breath (spirit) + Energy (His spoken word) => Man + Faith.

understanding of the vital existence of the Lord Jesus in our life by using "light" as the metaphor.

Similarly, David Jeremiah[32] once explained how the antichrist can achieve his control over the entire human population, possibly by implanting a silicon IC (integrated circuit) chip under each individual's skin to identify each person, as described in the book of Revelation (13:16–17, NIV). Please note that these are Bible teachers and scholars talking to their congregations, hoping the illustration can help the *modern* audiences grasp the essence of the Bible better in today's terminology. A modern audience knows that one grain-sized silicon chip can store a document of more than a million letters (one megabytes) and that the technology today enables us to store a person's identification, résumé from birth, and even a lifetime medical history in one chip. Therefore, storing the three letters like "666" and scan with radio waves to detect the number is a simple matter for a modern audience to perceive.

The point is that we cannot know God with our own understanding, unless God reveals Himself to us. And God reveals Himself to humanity according to the level of knowledge that they have gained at the time. After all, writers of the Scripture had to use the vocabularies that they knew to describe God's revelation in words that the readers of their era could understand. Consequently, we cannot expect to find in the Bible

---

32 The pastor and preacher of Shadow Mountain Community Church and the "Turning Point" TV ministry, El Cajon, CA

the modern vocabularies, such as photons, phonons, electrons, positively charged holes in P-type semiconductors, black holes in galaxies, etc. Therefore, in many cases, we have to read the Bible with different perspectives, instead of jumping to the wrong conclusion that the creation described in the first book of the Bible is a mythology and go astray from faith.

Our Frail and Feeble Mind

Human as we are, we tend to confine our beliefs only to the things that we can see, hear, taste, smell, or touch and do not easily change our mind-set to believe in things that are beyond our five senses. For example, we have been taught since our kindergarten days that 1+1+1=3. Now if someone tells us that 1+1+1=1 is also true, it would be hard for us to swallow.

However, in 1847 an English mathematician, George Boole (1815–1864), formulated a set of fundamental rules, 0+0=0, 0+1=1, 1+0=1, 1+1=1; 0•0=0, 0•1=0, 1•0=0, 1•1=1 and 1= ~ 0, from which axioms, theorems, and laws, were derived to become a branch of mathematics called Boolean algebra.[33] In the course of some 160 years and contributions of countless scientists and engineers, more branches of mathematics and applications were born, such as combinatorial mathematics, symbolic logic, set theory, switching theory, computer science and engineering, etc.

---

33 The "+" sign in computer logic is also represented by symbols, "OR" or "U for Union" and the symbol "•" is also represented by symbol "AND" or "∩ for Intersection", and "= ~" for "NOT" or "Negation" operation.

We do not question why or how, regarding the basic Boolean rules. But electronic engineers have studied and implemented these mathematical operations into switching circuits, which led to the development of computer hardware. And computer scientists have made use of these rules to implement system software as well as application software to make the hardware operational. As a result computers and communications have been in the vanguard of a digital revolution in human civilization.

Now we can use computers in all sorts of applications: seeing video images of faraway relatives and talking with them simultaneously on our PC; synthesizing complex molecules in the pharmaceutical and petrochemical industries; guiding automotive navigation with satellite-based GPS; surveying oil and mineral deposits from satellites in space; simulating and predicting earthquakes and weather patterns—just to mention a few. However, we must keep in mind that we are only the end users of computers. We can enjoy the computers without understanding the Boolean algebra or computer science. We never have to question the validity of the basic Boolean rules, for their vast applications have demonstrated their validity.

Those who are familiar with real number arithmetic may have to make a drastic change in mind-set to accept abstract mathematics. For example, if you ask "A+" students in high school algebra to accept the concept of eigenvectors in an infinite-dimensional space in advanced linear algebra, they will tell you it is indeed hard to comprehend.

For yet another example, those who can enjoy realistic paintings, such as *La gioconda* (*Mona Lisa*) by Leonardo da Vinci, may have to scratch their heads trying to figure out what the modern abstract paintings represent, such as *Lavender Mist* by Jackson Pollock or *One Year the Milkweed* by Arshile Gorky.

What is the point? The point is that some people who have *some* knowledge of science and accept this physical world may not be able to open their hearts to see and believe in the spiritual world. But the fact is that the existence of the unseen world is as real as quantum mechanics to the students of classical physics.

From these analogies, we may be able to perceive the creation in the Bible up to the level of knowledge that God has bestowed upon humankind. God had set rules, principles, and laws to create and sustain the universe, and we call them the laws of nature. We never have to question His existence, for the splendor of His creation speaks for itself (Ps. 19:1).

Atheists and agnostics give credit to the so-called laws of nature for everything and deny the existence and the work of God. This is as if the people who enjoy using computers dismissed the existence of scientists and engineers who laid the foundation for computer science and engineering. Some people boast their proficiency in computer skills and fail to recognize that they are only the end users. Likewise, some unbelievers boast of their knowledge of science and fail to recognize that they are just the end users of the God-made rules governing nature. I believe that if we cannot understand the genesis of the universe portrayed in the Bible, it is not because the Bible is nonscientific, but because we do not completely understand *both the Scripture and the science* with our frail and feeble minds, as Einstein put it. Science should draw us closer to our Creator, and no one should reject Him in the name of science.

Having said all the above, let me share my humble insights on the creation account in the Bible from different perspectives, which may have been overlooked by many prominent believer-scientists in their works.[34]

In Genesis 1:1–5 (NIV), the Bible says,

> [1] In the beginning God created the heavens and the earth. [2] Now the earth was formless and empty, darkness was over the surface of the deep, and the Spirit of God was hovering over the waters.
>
> [3] And God said, "Let there be light," and there was light.
>
> [4] God saw that the light was good, and He separated the light from the darkness. [5] God called the light "day," and the darkness he called

---

34 Gerald L. Schroeder, *Genesis and the Big Bang, The Science of God* (Broadway Books, 1997); Paul Davies, *God & the New Physics* (Touchstone, Simon & Schuster, 1983); Hugh Ross, *The Fingerprint of God* (Promise Publishing, 1989).

"night." And there was evening, and there was morning—the first day.

Let's examine *each word* as in the following.

In the Beginning

Verse 1 clearly states that the universe had a beginning, but people accepted this fact only after the observation of red shifts in the absorption spectra of stars in distant galaxies (meaning spectral lines shifted toward the red as compared to their proper positions representing wavelengths in a spectrometer). Since then scientists have *discarded* the old model that the universe was in a steady state without beginning and end. But now they *accept* a model that the universe is expanding at a high speed.

The projection of space and time back into the past from this continuing expansion has led scientists to conclude that this universe must have started from a single point of origin, the *singularity* (a geometric point that has no dimension, implying conditions under which the laws of our physics do not apply). The tremendous force that created the expanding universe makes the scientists conclude that in the beginning there had to be an explosion of a scale beyond human imagination. Thus the name *big bang model* was born.

Plausibly, the Bible has been telling us that the universe had a beginning all along for more than 4,000 years, but we had to wait to realize that fact until the discovery of the Doppler effect of wave phenomena and the knowledge to design optical instrumentation. In the future, as human knowledge progresses to an even higher level, the scientists may have to *modify* their models again, but the statement of Genesis 1:1 will *never need* modification. It sufficiently demonstrates the conciseness and time-invariant nature of the Bible.

We have mentioned the big bang model of creation postulated by scientists. In order to perceive how the big bang model may support the Bible, let us try to explain it in nontechnical terms.

In a billiard game, a player gives a shot at a white cue ball with a stick. The cue ball, having gained speed and momentum from the shot, collides with a cluster of balls, the *target*. Initially, the target balls are *packed* together, and the player cannot identify the number on each individual colored ball in the pile. After the collision with a *bang*, the target balls are scattered like an explosion by the impact of the cue ball, so the player can identify each ball's number, and the game starts from there. Scientists in high-energy particle physics play a similar game on a much larger scale with much smaller cue balls.

What are the differences? In the billiard game, if you make the cue ball hit the target so fiercely that one of the balls cracks open, you have to pay to replace it. But if you are a high-energy particle physicist who succeeds in cracking open a target ball and identifies new constituent particles in it, you may become a candidate for a Nobel Prize in physics.

In the billiard game, you use a cue stick to accelerate the white cue ball. In high-energy particle physics, scientists use a tunnel several miles long, mounted with electromagnets to synchronously accelerate the flying cue ball until it attains energy of more than one tera–electron volt (1 TeV). The prefix *tera-* represents a factor of ten to the twelfth power (10^{12})—that is, 1 followed by twelve zeros. The cue ball in this case is a beam of electrically charged particles, such as ions, protons, positrons,[35] or other exotic particles.

There are two types of accelerator colliders: the linear type, in which an injected beam is accelerated through a linear tunnel to collide with a target at the other end of the tunnel;[36] and the ring type, in which two injected beams are accelerated in circular paths in opposite directions to collide with each other.[37] The game is to crack open the targets to study their *fundamental* (or *elementary*) constituents and the types of forces that bind the constituents together to form matters and antimatters. So far, many exotic particle and antiparticle pairs have been discovered, but physicists have listed only six types of quarks

---

35 A positron or anti-electron is an antimatter counterpart of an electron. When a positron collides with an electron, mutual annihilation occurs.

36 The SLAC (Stanford Linear Accelerator Collider) National Accelerator Laboratory in California has a linear tunnel 2.4 miles long to accelerate the beam of injected particles.

37 The FNAL (Fermi National Accelerator Laboratory), in Illinois, USA, uses a ring structure 3.9 miles in circumference to accelerate; the LHC (Large Hadron Collider) in Geneva, Switzerland, also uses a ring-type accelerator 17 miles in circumference.

and leptons and six types of their antiparticle counterparts in what is known as the standard model. These are considered to be the building blocks of all matters and antimatters.[38]

Concluding from the experiments observed in the laboratory, the scientists postulated that billions of years ago, a mysterious energy that was huge beyond human imagination cracked open a point of singularity. This event literally tore up the nothingness, the "0," and the explosion generated trillions of elementary particles "+m" and antiparticles "−m" (as if $0 \rightarrow [+m] + [-m]$). This description supports the apostle Paul's description of God, "who gives life to the dead and *calls into existence the things that do not exist*" (Rom. 4:17, ESV, emphasis added). It has to be a supernatural being, God, who detonated the explosion and provided this enormous energy!

Scientists, however, even if they believe in God, cannot mention the word "God" in academic journals. For the mention of the Almighty makes the paper nonscientific and non-publishable in the secular community. At the other extreme, the mention of science to explain the Scripture seems to be taken as blasphemy

---

38 To learn more, see Web sites of each National Accelerator Laboratory. LHC is an international laboratory.

in the super-religious fundamentalist community.[39] Nevertheless, I believe science is the gift of God for humans to perceive His work through revelation in the Bible.

One more thing: we ask, "How could the writer, supposedly Moses, know the creation process to describe it in the Bible?" It has to be the One, the Creator of the universe, who showed the writer in a vision. *Thus, we can only use our present knowledge and terminology to perceive what Moses must have seen in the vision, just as Bible scholars interpret the vision that the Lord showed the apostle John in the book of Revelation.*

God Created the Heavens and the Earth.

Now, let us come back to Genesis 1:1–5. The first question we ask is how the big bang model supports the biblical description of the creation, for the big explosion does not seem to be recorded in the Scripture. But it is recorded in verses 1 and 2.

---

39 To those who object to explaining Scripture with science, allow me to remind them that Matthew wrote a Gospel targeted to a Jewish audience, Luke's to Greeks, and John's to both, as well as to people of Eastern cultures by addressing the Lord Jesus Christ as "the Word." And the Lord Jesus told Nicodemus, who believed salvation came by obeying the Law that he must be born again to believe in salvation by faith. Jesus did not tell the Samaritan woman by Jacob's well to be born again but told her to drink the living water that the Lord could offer. In other words, the Lord explains the same truth with different words, according to His audience's background and circumstances. I hope this would justify using scientific explanations to *modern* seekers, as well as people in the science and engineering professions.

First, the explosion was silent. Sound propagates through media such as gas, liquid, and solid, but there was nothing to support the propagation of sound in the beginning, before creation. Thus the Bible does not have to mention the explosion. The writer of Genesis could not have heard the sound of an explosion in the vision of the big bang, just as present-day astronomers can observe but cannot hear the *sound* of the birth of new stars and the death of old stars in distant nebulae.[40]

Some seekers ask, if new stars are being born every day as in NASA's reports, indicating that creation is still going on, this is contrary to the Bible which says that the creation of the universe was completed in six days. To answer this question, I think we can draw from the example from human creation. God made the first man, Adam, from dust (not by human birth)—that is, Adam was created. But the making of descendents from Adam and Eve by human birth is called reproduction, not creation. In other words, if we call the *creation* of the universe the big bang, we may call the *reproduction* of stars in nebulae "little bangs."

Thus, the birth of new stars does not contradict the Bible. It seems the universe is very much alive, just like the living creatures on earth; stars are born and stars die. Does God continue to govern and sustain the universe and everything in it? Of course He does. The Lord Jesus said, "My Father is working until now, and I Myself am working" (John 5:17).

---

40 A nebula (from Latin: "cloud"; pl. *nebulae* or *nebulas*) is an interstellar cloud of dust, hydrogen gas, helium gas, and plasma.

After the instant that God created space-time by the big bang, measurement of time and space was made possible. But it does not have to be the universe that is filled with today's cosmic bodies, stars, planets, and galaxies. This is amazingly described in verse 2, which says, "Now the earth was formless and empty, darkness was over the surface of the deep, and the Spirit of God was hovering over the waters."

Now the Earth Was Formless and Empty

The word *now* indicates the time immediately after the big bang. The statement "the earth was formless and empty" tells us that the infant universe did not have stars or planets, not even molecules. Rather, it was filled with trillions and trillions of leptons and quarks. Leptons are electrons, muons, tauons, and their respective neutrinos. Quarks have six different kinds. There are up, down, charm, strange, top, and bottom quarks, not to mention the corresponding anti-leptons and anti-quarks.

Beloved readers please do not be intimidated by these scientific names. I am sure God has different names for these particles, and He is kind enough not to tell us in the Bible so as to avoid confusing us.

Similarly, we should not be intimidated by the terminology used by religious scholars, such as eschatology, soteriology, hamartiology, pneumatology, Christology, bibliology, and theology.[41]

41 John F. MacArthur, *The Second Coming* (Crossway Books, 1999), 20.

"The earth was formless" means that these elementary particles had not yet formed to become atoms or molecules at this stage of universe.

I think the word *empty* can have two possible meanings:

It is describing how small the elementary particles are. The mass of each particle is in the range of 10^{-25} to 10^{-35} kilograms. The number 10^{-35} means "one divided by the quantity written out as 1 followed by 35 zeros." For example, neutrinos, which have no electric charge and are ten thousand times smaller than electrons, can pass through any matter. The neutrinos that are emitted from the sun are believed to pass right through our bodies as if traveling though an *empty* space.

Apart from the word *empty*, how else can we expect the writer of the Scripture to describe the smallness of the particles in his era? He did not have the scientific notation system of our days. Even in our modern days, I wonder how much of the world population is familiar with metric prefixes such as mega- (10^6), giga- (10^9), tera- (10^{12}), peta- (10^{15}), and exa- (10^{18}), to describe huge numbers. Thank God for sparing us from these notations in the Bible. The Bible is meant for all mankind, not just for the scientists. (*Thou shall not take the loving kindness of thy God as nonscientific.*)

Another possible meaning of the word *empty* is a reference to the dual properties of matter. Matter can show itself as a particle as well as a wave (when the matter is traveling at near light speed). A particle is defined by its size, its mass, and its position, but a wave has no size, mass, or position to measure. However, a wave can be defined by its amplitude, its frequency, and the energy that it carries and its position can be measured when standing waves form a wave packet. So the infant universe is filled with something that can be literally described as "Now you see it (particles), and now you don't (wave radiation)." And even in particle form, they are too small to see with human eyes, unless God zoomed in the particles for Moses to see. How can we expect Moses to describe this concept except with the word *empty*?

More important, could it be that the knowledge of the dual properties of matter in *modern physics* is a gift of God, so that we can *metaphysically*[42] perceive the validity of much more complex multiple properties—body, soul, and spirit in a human—and God expressed in multiple persons, Father, Son, and Holy Spirit in one triune God? (We shall discuss this subject in the next chapter.)

Darkness Was Over the Surface of the Deep

This verse is an even more amazing statement supported by science. I believe the word *surface* refers to the boundary that separates our physical universe from the region where space-

---

42 *Metaphysics* is defined in the Merriam-Webster Dictionary as: (a) a division of philosophy that is concerned with the fundamental nature of reality and being and that includes ontology, cosmology, and often epistemology; (b) abstract philosophical studies: a study of what is outside objective experience. (It is not a quantitative study like physical science.)

time has not yet extended, which is described as *the darkness* in the Scripture. This statement implies that the universe has a *finite* size and is expanding at a *finite* speed. If photons (light) had infinite speed, space-time would have covered all darkness of the deep, and there would be no *surface* at all. But the universe has finite size, and the Scripture accurately describes that there is a *surface* enclosing the universe. Beyond this boundary surface is a region unknowable by us, the *depth* of which is beyond our imagination. After the big bang, space-time was created within the universe and beyond the surface of the expanding universe, there is no concept of space-time to measure the depth in the first place. How much more scientific can we ask the Bible to be?

The big bang model says that the expanding universe is like a balloon being inflated. Points on the surface of the balloon move apart, but none of them is the center of expansion. Galaxies that we see behave as if they were embedded on the *surface* of an inflating balloon. As the balloon is inflating at an accelerating rate, the distances between galaxies on the balloon's surface are increasing (showing red shift), but each individual galaxy itself is not spreading. (This is one of the many mysteries that led scientists to postulate the existence of dark matter and dark energy.) Taking the balloon analogy, the surface of a balloon separates the gas inside from the outside of the balloon. Thus the big bang model does support the Bible.

We should ask how the writer of the Scripture, who did not have our modern scientific knowledge, knew all these things—the fast but finite speed of photons, the finite speed at which the finite universe expands, and the description of a boundary *surface*! Unless it was someone who was there and created the universe and revealed it to man in a vision, the writer of the Scripture could not possibly have written about the creation processes so precisely. Recalling this same question over and over again and one cannot refuse to believe, as I did, that the Bible is indeed the Book inspired by a supernatural Being, God (see 2 Tim. 3:16).

The Spirit of God Was Hovering Over the Waters

Another question that some seekers ask is, "What did the writer see in the God-revealed vision regarding this verse?" To me, the best answers are "I don't know, because I wasn't there" and "the Christian faith is to believe what the Scripture says". But you have guessed it; such an answer would never satisfy our seekers in the science and engineering professions. Thus, let us illustrate the parallel or similarity between the physical and spiritual worlds.

By the burst of a big explosion, God literally tore open the nothingness and created pairs of elementary particles and antiparticles as mentioned earlier. Here, I believe that the word "*waters*" does not necessarily mean H_2O, for molecules were not yet formed, until the second day. The infant universe was filled with swarms of elementary particles, which *flow past the observer* like streams of fluid. "*Waters*" was probably the only word that the writer could use to describe what was seen in the vision.

In our modern terminology, we classify the *states of matter* as solid, liquid, gas, and plasma[43] (we do not have words for the *states* of dark matter yet, that is if it exists as the scientists postulate.) Since all the elementary particles, with the exception of neutrinos, possess electric charges and the movement of charged particles generates magnetic fields. Thus the infant universe was filled with plasma of charged particles and electromagnetic radiations rather than H_2O molecules.

The Spirit of God is invisible to humans, and God had to show Moses with something that he could see and describe in the Bible for people to read. I believe that "hovering over the waters" means something moving over trillions of charged particles in a plasma state. Something close to this description in our present-day knowledge is the aurora, or northern or southern lights,

---

43 Wikipedia, the free encyclopedia, on *plasma* (physics): "In physics and chemistry, plasma is a gas in which a certain portion of the particles are ionized. The presence of a non-negligible number of charge carriers makes the plasma electrically conductive so that it responds strongly to electromagnetic fields. Plasma, therefore, has properties quite unlike those of solids, liquids, or gases and is considered to be a distinct state of matter. Like gas, plasma does not have a definite shape or a definite volume unless enclosed in a container; unlike gas, in the influence of a magnetic field, it may form structures such as filaments, beams and double layers. Some common plasmas are flame, lightning, and the Sun." (Wikipedia)

which display a hovering, shimmering luminescence in the sky. The Cree tribes in northern Canada call it "dance of the spirits", and in the fourteenth century, the auroras were called a sign from God (Wilfried Schröder, *Das Phänomen des Polarlichts*, Darmstadt, 1984).

Again the important question is how Moses could describe the vision. He might have seen mirages in the desert, but he could not have possibly seen the aurora in his lifetime, because it is an astrophysical phenomenon that can occur only in the regions near earth's poles, where there are relatively strong magnetic fields. I am not suggesting that Moses saw the aurora, but I believe he saw something in a vision that he never saw in his life, and I cannot help but believe that it was a supernatural God who inspired Moses to write the Scriptures through that vision.

We must keep it in mind that the aurora-like phenomena itself is not the Spirit of God. It is God's way of showing His presence, just as He used a column of cloud by day and a column of fire by night to lead the Israelites after they had left Egypt. The column of cloud or fire itself was not God. It was God's way of showing His presence, assuring the Israelites that they were not alone, He was there to lead them. Here it is showing the presence of God in the creation of the universe.

Another physical phenomenon that Moses possibly saw in the vision was the mutual annihilation of particles and antiparticles. (When such paired particles collide, they annihilate each other.

In the process, the masses of the trillions and trillions of these particle pairs convert back to energetic radiation of different wavelengths, some can be in the visible range like *lightning*.) And those other trillions of electrically charged leptons and quarks that survived annihilation soon combined to form heavier particles, such as protons and neutrons, and eventually became atoms and molecules, according to the *rules* set by God.[44] Again, there had to be a supernatural Being who revealed all these to the writer of Genesis who saw the vision. Thus the big bang model supports the vision in the Scripture which says, "The Spirit of God was hovering over the waters."

And God Said, "Let There Be Light," and There Was Light

So continues the Scripture in verse 3.

A critic asked, "In verse 2, if Moses saw the charged particles, radiations, plasmas, aurora-like hovering light and possibly lightning, why didn't he mention light in verse 2? Vocabulary could not be the problem; Moses certainly knew the word *light* even in his time. Why did he wait until verse 3 to mention it?"

It is a good question! But I believe there are two reasons to do so: (1) According to scientist's estimation, it took 10^{-34}

---

44 We do not have to ask "why" regarding God's rules—conversion taking place interchangeably between energy and mass, the magnetic forces generated by moving electrical charges, the weak force that makes higher energy particles decay, the strong force that binds the elementary particles to form atoms and molecules, etc.—just as we do not ask why $1+1+1=3$ in arithmetic and $1+1+1=1$ in Boolean algebra.

second for the big bang to generate the infant universe filled with elementary particles. Thus the events in verses 2 and 3 occurred at practically the same time. Yet, in writing, two simultaneous events cannot be described by a single line but by two lines in succession. (2) The author of Genesis had to *explicitly* reiterate that the first thing God created was *light* in verse 3, for the entire sequence of six-day creation followed this verse. The author could not describe the entire sequence by omitting the mention of the first thing that was created. Besides, without "light" first, no creature could sustain life.

God knew what He was doing, and the narration of the Scripture is very scientifically logical. Basically, verse 2 indicates the presence of God and that He detonated the big bang. Verse 3 tells us that the first thing He created was "light" and that He created it by His spoken word.

God Has Spoken

In verse 1:3, when God said, "Let there be light" His thought possessed tremendous energy, and His spoken word had enormous power, transforming His thought into physical actuality, the heavens and the earth. This is not that difficult for us to perceive, because God created us in His own image (Gen. 1:26–27), and as a result, we have the ability to think and speak. Among all the creatures on earth, only human beings can reason logically, analyze complex problems, and represent their thoughts in spoken words, texts, drawings, static pictures, dynamic animations, or even three-dimensional holograms.

When we are thinking hard, our brain waves are much more active (shown in frequencies) and intense (amplitude) than when we are sound asleep. Thus we are also emitting energies from our thoughts. However, our brain waves are of very low frequencies (long wavelengths), from a low end of 1.5 to 4 Hz ("Hertz" represents cycles per second), called "delta waves", and up to a high end of 15 to 40 Hz, called "beta waves."[45] Since wave energy is proportional to wave frequency, the energy emitted by our brain is very insignificant as compared to gamma radiation, which has frequencies as high as 2.9×10^{27} Hz (one million billion trillion times more energetic than human brain waves).

I mention this number only to show how infinitesimally small the energy that our thoughts can radiate. On the other hand, we can never imagine a number big enough to represent the illimitable energy and power that the thought of God possesses. The energy of human brain waves is so small that it can only be detected by a man-made instrument called the electroencephalograph (EEG). The thought of God is so illimitably great that it cannot be detected by any man-made device. Even gamma ray photons can be detected only after men's discovery of Campton Scattering phenomenon and

---

45 Brain waves are classified in 4 types: beta, alpha, theta, and delta, listed in the decreasing order of wave frequencies, according to the state of mind (from actively thinking to sound sleep). Please do not confuse them with alpha and beta particle emission in nuclear physics (Terminology can be a tower of Babel in science.)

the invention of sensors, photomultipliers, and charge-coupled semiconductor devices.

God's thought can be detected only by inspiration through the work of Holy Spirit. It is a very sophisticated mechanism beyond our imagination.

With recent advances in wireless sensory apparatus, researchers can track four channels of brainwave patterns (beta, alpha, theta, and delta waves) and use pattern recognition technology to remotely control the cursor movement on a computer screen with human thought.[46] Thus, it is not so difficult for us to perceive that God can turn His thought into matter and energy. Perhaps, we can perceive the greatness of energy in His spoken Word by the equation $E=mc^2$, where m is the mass of the entire universe (which is too large for us to imagine), c is the speed of light (about 300,000,000 meters/sec), and E is the energy carried by the thought of the Almighty, and this is only for the creation of the universe that we think we know.

Thus, the Lord God says:

> "My thoughts are not your thoughts,
>
> neither are your ways my ways,"
>
> declares the LORD.
>
> "As the heavens are higher than the earth,
>
> so are my ways higher than your ways

---

46 In addition to the detection of temporal patterns of brain waves, a set of more than three sensors enable detection of spatial patterns of our thought to move or operate physical instrument or machines. (see Tan Le, *A headset that reads your brainwaves*, July 22, 2010 TED presentation, http:/ www.ted.com).

and my thoughts than your thoughts."

–(Isaiah 55:8–9, NIV)

Speaking of the parallel between spiritual and physical worlds, God made a short and simple declaration: "Let there be light" and *there was light.* The result of God's spoken word was instantaneous. Spiritually, this shows God's sovereign power over nature; physically, it adds the nuance of showing how fast the spoken word of God is transformed into materialization. In his book, Stephen Hawking wrote that it took 10^{-34} second for the big bang to generate elementary particles and 10^{-10} second for these particles to form protons, neutrons, and mesons. Totally, it took only three minutes from the explosion to the stage where the infant universe was filled with matter and radiation *coupled* together.[47] This universe was indeed created by a short but powerful Word of God.

The Scripture goes on to say,

> [4] God saw that the light was good, and He separated the light from the darkness. [5] God called the light "day," and the darkness he called "night." And there was evening, and there was morning—the first day.

---

47 Hawking, *Brief History of Time*, 149.

God Saw that the Light Was Good

Genesis 1:4 tells us that God has feelings; otherwise, we humans wouldn't have them, for He created humankind in His image. He felt good when He saw light. The question is what could have happened if He didn't like it? Simple, He could just let the matter and antimatter annihilate each other, and everything would have returned to the nothingness. Thank God that He liked it, and we are here as a result.

This may be one scientific perspective on the scripture "God is love" and "We love because He first loved us" (1 John 4:19). And if you ask how much, John 3:16 is the answer. Because God liked what He saw, the next step that the Almighty took follows in the same verse: He separated the light from the darkness.

And He Separated the Light from the Darkness

In this same verse the word *darkness* appears again. Amazingly, the writer of Genesis seemed to know the difference between the *darkness* here in the second part of verse 4 and the *darkness* in verse 2, where it says "darkness was over the surface of the deep." God told the writer of Genesis the difference, so that it was important enough for him to *repeat* the word. The first *darkness* (v. 2) is in reference to the nothingness *outside* the boundary *surface* of the universe, where space-time has not reached yet. The second *darkness* (v. 4) denotes the dark regions *on* and *inside* the boundary surface where space-time has already appeared.

The darkness here in verse 4 is not nothingness but rather is filled with something unknown to man. It is not visible to human eyes or detectable with instruments. Thus, the scientists have *postulated* an unknown substance and call it "dark matter" and "dark energy," which will be discussed in the chapter on the second day of creation in this book.

The Scripture continues:

> God called the light "day," and the darkness he called "night." And there was evening, and there was morning—the first day. (Gen. 1:5, NIV)

Since the solar system was made on the fourth day (see Genesis 1:14–19), verse 1:5 is not likely talking about our solar system; this is clear from the second day of creation. What did the writer see in the vision then? I believe God set the universe into motion. The writer saw that all the particles in the infant universe were spinning about their own axes, and at the same time revolving around each other so that they could avoid colliding with their antiparticle counterparts and being annihilated. Again, the Scripture is very logically ordered: God created light first, so the writer could see the light-side and the dark-side of particles. In other words, the writer is describing that the entire universe created by God is dynamic. I believe the writer did not have the vocabulary for "periodic motion" to describe spinning objects. God exercised His authority to give the name *day* to one side of a spinning particle that the writer saw in the vision—an atom, a molecule, and eventually a cosmic body—and to name the opposite side *night*.

The First Day

Regarding the definition of a day (Heb. *yom*) in the six days of creation, there are many arguments between believers and unbelievers and even among believers.

- Apologists for a literal sense believe that each day is literally a 24-hour earthly day, and God created the universe in six 24-hour earthly days.

- Skeptics call this portrayal of a six-day creation in the Bible a myth, because they believe the age of the universe is about 13.7 billion years, and the first stars were formed about 200 million years after the big bang, according to scientific estimates.

- Gerald L. Schroeder[48] points out that the writer of Genesis may have used different time units to measure events before and after the creation of man. To be specific, it was on the sixth day that God created man, so that "day" is expressed in the creation-day unit. After the creation, Adam lived to one hundred and

---

48 *Genesis and the Big Bang.*

thirty years, and this is based on the post-creation unit which is earthly-24-hour days.

As for me, I believe the "one day" in the six-day creation can mean three seconds, thirteen billion years, or twenty-four earthly hours.

How so?

(1) The first day in the Scripture can mean less than three seconds. God's declaration shows instant results. He said "Let there be light," and there was light. Scientists say that it took less than three seconds from the big bang for the infant universe to be filled with particles and radiation.

(2) The second day in the Scripture can mean thirteen billion years to create the Milky Way and other galaxies from cosmic dust, nebulas, and the birth of stars.

I believe that the passage is the narration of what the writer saw in his vision, and it is the writer's 24-hour earthly day. Although the creation, from big bang to the formation of the infant universe, took place in less than three seconds, it took the writer a 24-hour day to view the playback of the creation: the big bang, generation of the infant universe filled with all sorts of fundamental particles, the mutual annihilation of particles and their antiparticle counterparts, and visible light as well as invisible radiation in a vision. In other words, God showed the entire creation process in visions spread over six sessions, and the writer saw each session as one 24-hour earthly day.

(3) In fact, the Scripture counts "the first day", "the second day" and so on and never mentions the length of each day. This alone convinces me that the Scripture is not talking about the time God took in the creation process, but it is the writer's counting of the event he observed each day. Because the writer saw the solar system only on the fourth day, and before that there was no definition of earthly day as yet. It never ceases to amaze me that the Scripture is so scientifically accurate that it avoids defining the length of each day in the creation process, because billions of years ago, one spin of our earth was not necessarily the 24 hours of a current earthly day; the planet spun faster. If this interpretation is acceptable, there would be *no need for argument.*

Scientists estimate that the age of the universe is about 13.75 ± 0.17 billion years, meaning that the accuracy of the estimation allows an error of 170 million years. The error may be a small number in cosmology, but if we compare it with Adam's 130 years of life on earth, it does not make sense to me to argue about how long God took to create the universe with human understanding. Therefore, I would just take it as the Scripture says: God created the universe in six days, because the Bible does not explain in detail about it, and we can only imagine the vision Moses saw.

7. Science Is a Gift of God (II) –Trinity
John 1:1–5

—————————— ❧ ——————————

[To you Christians] who have been chosen according to the foreknowledge of God the Father, through the sanctifying work of the Spirit, for obedience to Jesus Christ and sprinkling by his blood: Grace and peace be yours in abundance. (1 Peter 1:2, NIV)

The Trinity refers to the Christian understanding of God as a unity of three persons: Father, Son, and Holy Spirit. All are equally God and so One, each sharing in the divine attributes of ultimacy, eternity, and changelessness; yet they are distinguishable in their relations to each other and in their roles within creaturely and human life and destiny.

—Langdon Gilkey (1919–2004), University of Chicago theologian

The Trinity—namely God in three Persons, the Father, the Son, and the Holy Spirit yet One God—is a very difficult concept for some to understand. Although theologians and Bible scholars have written many books and essays[49] attempting to explain the meaning of the Trinity, it remains incomprehensible in the minds of many.

According to Ron Rhodes,[50] Jehovah's Witnesses are famous for their denial of the Trinity, a denial based on these points: (1) There is no word "Trinity" in the Bible, so it is not biblical. (2) The Old Testament says, "There is only one God," so Jesus Christ cannot be God. There are many well-written essays debating against these misunderstandings, notably by Ron Rhodes and James White.[51]

While Bible scholars are debating from a religious perspective, allow me to share my perception of the Trinity from a scientific perspective and claim that science is a gift of God for men to understand Him better—even the concept of the Trinity.

---

49 Countless books and discussions can be found in Google search with key words "Christian Faith, Trinity". Newer published books that the author knows include Robert Letham, *The Holy Trinity, In Scripture, History, Theology, and Worship* (P&R Publishing, 2004); and Tom Bosse, *The Unveiling of the Trinity* (Tuvott Publishing, 2003).
A summary of essays on the Trinity by many prominent theologians and scholars can be found at http://mb-soft.com/believe/text/trinity.htm.
50 Ron Rhodes, "The Trinity: The Case Study in Implicit Truth," *Christian Research Journal*, vol. 29, number 1 (2006).
51 James R. White, "Loving the Trinity," *Christian Research Journal*, vol. 21, number 4 (1999).

Nature Shows Concept of Trinity

When God created the universe, the first thing He created was light. Jesus metaphorically referred Himself as "Light." And amazingly enough, light itself shows characteristics that evoke the concept of trinity (three in one).

Isaac Newton (1643–1727), an English physicist, mathematician, astronomer, natural philosopher, and theologian, demonstrated the light spectrum by passing a white light[52] beam through a prism to display *three* primary colors and three secondary colors of light. As the science progressed, we now know that all *visible* light can be *additively* composed with three lights in the primary colors—red, green, and blue light (RGB). Engineers have made use of this principle, and now we can enjoy color televisions in every home.

I believe the principle that white light is composed of three primary colors can be used as a metaphor or symbol to help us perceive the concept of the Trinity. Since followers of Judaism and Jehovah's Witnesses do not believe in the Trinity (but I assume they know Isaac Newton's experiment), I hope they do not object to the following equation:

---

52 Some people refer to sunlight as colorless light, but Isaac Newton called it white light in his book *Opticks* (1704). Colorless can mean black to some people.

White light (let it be the symbol for *One God, the Triune*[53]) =

Blue light (symbol for *God, the Father*)

+ Green light (symbol for *God, the Holy Spirit*)

+ Red light (symbol for "**?**")

Where "+" is additive of light components. We shall identify the third Person designated as "**?**".

Three in One

If one of the three primary RGB colors is missing, white light cannot be formed. Since this principle exists in God's creation, could it be that the Triune God is revealing His attribute of Trinity to us through this physical phenomenon? With this analogy, I believe we can comprehend that the existence of the third Person "**?**", as one of the three divine Persons, is absolutely essential in God, the Triune.

Coequal

In order to compose a *pure* white light, the three RGB components must be *equal* in intensity. Let BGR be the three

---

53 Instead of *Godhead*, we use the phrase *God, the Triune* here to avoid confusion for some Sunday school students who tend to associate the word *head* with the human body part and imagine a human head with three faces, as the ancient Greeks did.

elements[54] in a notation of finite sets, and "+" as "addition of light"; then

$$\text{Pure Blue } \{1,0,0\} + \text{Pure Green } \{0,1,0\} + \text{Pure}$$
$$\text{Red } \{0,0,1\} = \text{Pure White } \{1,1,1\}[55]$$

If any component is either less or more intense than the other two, the resultant light will not be *pure* white light. This property of light metaphorically reveals that the three Divine Persons must be *coequal*. Therefore, just as the three colors are uniquely distinguishable, and yet they combine to form one white light, so the Father, the Holy Spirit, and "?" are uniquely distinguishable, yet together One God.

---

54 Here, these primary colors are used to symbolize three Divine Persons: Blue as the Father, representing, among other attributes, power of God (imagine the ultraviolet ray, which can tell the difference between real and fake diamonds and other precious stones); Green as the Holy Spirit, representing, among other attributes, the tenderness of God (intercedes for us with groaning too deep for words; imagine how soothing green can be to human eyes); and Red as the Son, representing, among other attributes, the redeeming God (imagine the blood Jesus shed for humanity and the healing power of infrared). The conventional order, RGB, is counting from the outer to the inner color of rainbows and in the order of lower to higher frequencies of the light spectrum. Blue, Green, Red (BGR) is the order from higher to lower frequencies, and the three Divine Persons that these colors are chosen to represent appeared in the Bible in this order: the Father (B), the Holy Spirit (G), and the Son (R). Therefore, I employ RGB for physical light and BGR for spiritual symbols in this book.
55 In digital 8 bit color notation Blue={255,0,0}, Green={0,255,0}, Red={0,0,255} and White={255,255,255}.

Deity of the Third Person

Blue light is light, green light is light, and red light is light. Though distinguishable by their colors that are used as adjectives, light is light because these three components are physically all electromagnetic waves, distinguishable only by their wavelengths (or frequencies). That is why they can be merged to produce white light, which is also an electromagnetic wave. By analogy, the Father is God; the Holy Spirit is God; thus in order for the Triune God to be God, the third Person must be God. We Christians believe that this Third Person must be Jesus Christ, who is also a Divine Deity in the New Testament.

Coeternity

Since we accept that God is eternal (Isaiah 41:4; 43:10–11; 44:6, 24), the above two arguments assure us that all three Divine Persons must be eternal. Nevertheless, let us dig deeper into this attribute from another perspective.

When we talk about *eternity*, the factor of time is involved. Let us start with the New Testament, in which the Trinity is abundantly clear (Matt. 3:16–17; Matt. 28:19; John 14:16–17; 2 Cor. 13:14; Acts 2:32–33; John 10:30; 17:11, 21), and then trace back to the Old Testament. By so doing, we will understand why the Trinity is not explicitly mentioned in the Old Testament.

The New Testament

In the New Testament, let the three Divine Persons and their relationships be symbolically represented by the three colored circles and their overlapping areas as shown in the Venn diagram[56] of Figure 1.

> Blue circle, **B**= {everything the New Testament says about God, the Father},
>
> e.g., "But of that day and hour no one knows, not even the angels of heaven, nor the Son, but the Father alone." (Matt. 24:36);
>
> Green circle, **G**= {everything the New Testament says about God, the Holy Spirit},
>
> e.g., "And they were all filled with the Holy Spirit and began to speak with other tongues, as the Spirit was giving them utterance." (Acts 2:4)
>
> Red circle, **R**= {everything the New Testament says about God, the Son},

---

56 "Venn diagrams or set diagrams are diagrams that show all possible logical relations between finite collections of sets (groups of things). Venn diagrams were conceived around 1880 by John Venn. They are used to teach elementary set theory, as well as illustrate simple set relationships in probability, logic, statistics, linguistics, and computer science." (Wikipedia)

e.g., "And they all said, 'Are You the Son of God, then?' And He said to them, 'Yes, I am.'" (Luke 22:70)

Cyan, **C**= {everything the New Testament says about the relationship between the Father *and* the Holy Spirit}. In *logic notation*, it can be represented by intersection "∩" operation, **C=B∩G,**

e.g., "In the same way, the Spirit helps us in our weakness. We do not know what we ought to pray for, but the Spirit himself intercedes for us with groans that words cannot express." (Romans 8:26, NIV) (The passage is relating the Holy Spirit to the Father.)

Magenta, **M**={everything the New Testament says about the relationship between the Father *and* the Son}. In logic notation it can be represented by M= B∩R

e.g., "The Father loves the Son and has given all things into His hand." (John 3:35)

"He who has seen Me [the Son, Jesus Christ] has seen the Father; how can you say, 'Show us the Father'?" (John 14:9)

Yellow, **Y** = {everything the New Testament says about the relationship between the Son *and* the Holy Spirit}. It can be represented by Y=R∩G

e.g., "and who through the Spirit of holiness was declared with power to be the Son of God by his resurrection from the dead: Jesus Christ our Lord." (Romans 1:4, NIV)

White, **W** = {everything that the New Testament says about the relationships of three Persons: Father, Holy Spirit, *and* Son} can be represented by

W = (B∩G∩R)

e.g.

The Holy Spirit descended upon Him in bodily form like a dove, and a voice came out of heaven, 'You are My beloved Son, in You I am well-pleased.'" (Luke 3:22)

"Go therefore and make disciples of all the nations, baptizing them in the name of the Father and the Son and the Holy Spirit ..." (Matt. 28:19)

Then, everything that the New Testament says about each or all the Divine Persons and their relationships are the elements in the set covered by the union "U" of the three circles: All related to God **All = (BUGUR).**

All the logical relations stated above are represented by the following Venn diagram, Figure 1.

The Old Testament

In the New Testament, the three Divine Persons are individually distinguishable as illustrated in the above passages of Scripture, but in the Old Testament the three Persons are not explicitly mentioned. This situation can be illustrated as follows: Imagine the Blue, Green, and Red circles are getting closer together in the Venn diagram; the white color intersection increases in size. Ultimately, when the three circles totally overlap to become three concentric circles, the white intersection becomes a circle that is exactly the same size as any of the three circles. This is when the three colors (symbolically representing three divine Persons) become indistinguishable, and only one white circle (symbolically God the Triune) is visible. This means that in the Old Testament the three Persons are totally in accord in their attributes, thoughts, ways, and actions in the Trinity (Figure 2).

When RBG are blended thoroughly and become pure white, we cannot describe the light by the adjectives *blue*, *green*, and *red*, but by *white*. Similarly in this condition, we no longer need to describe the Divine Persons by the adjectives Father, Holy Spirit, or Son, but by One Triune God, in the Old Testament. The adjective *Triune* can be omitted by saying "One God," just as we call white light simply "light," omitting the adjective *white*.

This *condition* for three circles to become concentric circles (to completely overlap) can be described by Boolean logic as:

All $(B \cup G \cup R)$ = White $(B \cap G \cap R)$

Analogically,

If and only if

(Father) $\cup$ (Holy-Spirit) $\cup$ (Son) = (Father) $\cap$ (Holy-Spirit) $\cap$ (Son)

Then

One God =

(Father) $\cup$ (Holy-Spirit) $\cup$ (Son) =

(The Father) = (The Holy-Spirit) = (The Son).

This means that the three Persons and the relations among them are indistinguishably close. I believe this is the case in the Old Testament—where, however, the One God is most often represented by God the Father or the Almighty.

Venn diagram of the Three Primary Colors

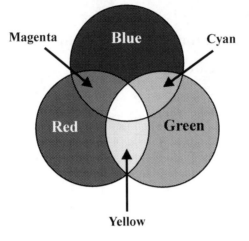

Additive (light)

Figure 1: Venn Diagram of additive RGB colors
See color representation on back cover.

Three Primary Colors & Symbolic representations

B= Blue — God, the Father

G= Green — God, the Holy Spirit

R= Red — God, the Son

Three Secondary Colors

C= Cyan =B∩G — Father and H. Spirit relationship

M=Magenta=B∩R — Father and Son relationship

Y=Yellow= G∩R — H. Spirit and Son relationship

W=White=B∩G∩R — The attributes of God, the Triune

A=All=B∪G∪R — Union of the Three Divine Persons
and their mutual relationships

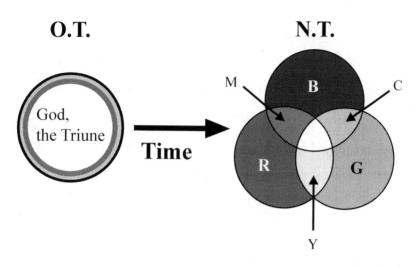

Figure 2: Trinity from Old Testament to New Testament

When $(B \cup G \cup R) = (B \cap G \cap R)$,

The three circles are concentric.

The three Divine Persons completely in accord in thoughts, ways, and action—indistinguishable in O.T.

The three Divine Persons become distinguishable in N.T after the birth of Christ for the salvation of mankind. However, their relationships remain, namely,

$(B \cap G \cap R = \sim 0)$.

Only through N.T. Do We See Trinity in O.T.

Just as we cannot look at the white light and tell that there are three primary colors in it without a prism to study it, we cannot tell that God is One God with three Divine Persons in the Old Testament without studying the New Testament. It is an amazing parallel of the spiritual and physical worlds. Isn't it one more reason for us to believe that science is a gift of God for men to perceive Him better?

Through Salvation of Mankind We See Trinity

What else can we infer? The three colors of light are revealed only when the white light interacts with physical matter (a prism). *Similarly*, the Triune God shows three distinguishable Persons only when God interacts with humanity for our salvation, and that is the case in the New Testament. In the Old Testament, the salvation was planned (Gen. 3:15), and it seems that there was as yet no need to show the Trinity explicitly. But in the New Testament the plans of the Triune God were executed by the ministry of Jesus Christ on earth, and that was the time the Trinity was explicitly made known. Just as it takes a *prism* for a white light to show three RGB components, it took 400 *silent years* for the Trinity (BGR) to be revealed in connection with the incarnation of Christ in the New Testament.

Is this explanation biblical? I believe it is. How else can we correlate the first five verses of the Gospel according to John with the first five verses of Genesis?

The Scripture says in the Gospel:

[1] In the beginning was the Word, and the Word was with God, and the Word was God

[2] He was in the beginning with God.

[3] All things came into being through Him, and apart from Him nothing came into being that has come into being.

[4] In Him was life, and the life was the Light of men.

[5] The Light shines in the darkness, and the darkness did not comprehend it. (John 1:1–5)

The phrase, "In the beginning" in verse 1 is the same beginning of time as in Genesis 1:1. "The Word" stands for Christ. I believe what John is trying to say in verse 2 is that "Although the Lord Jesus Christ is not mentioned explicitly, He was with the Father and the Holy Spirit." And the deity of Christ in the Trinity is explicit at the end of verse 1: "the Word was God."

Verse 3 means that just as light is vital to the life of all plants and living creatures, all things came into being through the Lord Jesus, and apart from Him, life in the universe is not sustainable. Verse 4 explicitly says that the Lord Jesus gave life to men and without Light (metaphorically, God the Son), men would perish. Verse 5 says that He is God in the Trinity, but men fallen in sins could not recognize Him and rejected Him, for they do not comprehend either the Light or the Trinity.

This straightforward interpretation of verse 5 is based on John 8:12–13:

> [12] Then Jesus again spoke to them, saying, "I am the Light of the world; he who follows Me will not walk in the darkness, but will have the Light of life."

> [13] So the Pharisees said to Him, "You are testifying about Yourself; Your testimony is not true."

People fallen in sins are walking in the darkness, since the days of Adam. Light came, and whoever accepts the Light will be saved– receiving life. But there are people, such as those Pharisees in verse 13, who refuse to accept Him, perhaps because they do not know or do not want to accept that Jesus is the Son of God, one of the Trinity. [For a more in-depth theological interpretation of John 1:1–5, the reader is invited to read some of the many books investigating such questions. The purpose of this section is to correlate John 1:1–5 with Genesis 1:1–5 and to identify Jesus Christ with the third Person in the Trinity.]

Correlation between O.T. and N.T.

Although the Trinity is implicit in the Old Testament, has God ever hinted that the three Persons would become distinguishable when the Triune God was ready to execute the work of salvation of humankind from sins? I believe He has. God said to Noah, "This is the sign of the covenant I am making between me and you and every living creature with you, a covenant for all generations to come" (Genesis 9:12, NIV). And what was the sign? The rainbow—white light refracted by water droplets, displaying multicolor rainbow.

> Whenever I bring clouds over the earth and the rainbow appears in the clouds, I will remember my covenant between me and you and all living creatures of every kind. Never again will the waters become a flood to destroy all life. Whenever the rainbow appears in the clouds, I will see it and remember the everlasting covenant between God and all living creatures of every kind on the earth. (Gen. 9:14–16, NIV)

God established the everlasting covenant between Himself and all earthly life with a multicolor rainbow as a sign. Can we see how this relates to the New Testament and to the illustration using the light spectrum?

- The rainbow is the sign of covenant, and the New Testament is also a covenant.

- The rainbow covenant was the (Old Testament) sign of promise that God would not wipe out humankind;

and the New Testament covenant is the fulfillment to save humankind from eternal damnation.

- Both the rainbow and the illustration here in this book use the visible light spectrum.

- Is it without foundation to illustrate with three primary colors in one white light to demonstrate the concept of the Trinity?

- Is it without foundation that I claim that science is a gift of God for us to know Him better by analogy? You be the judge.

8. Science Is a Gift of God (III) – Second Coming

> But of that day and hour no one knows, not even the angels of heaven, nor the Son, but the Father alone. (Matt. 24:36)

One member of a Bible study group asked, "If the Son doesn't know the day of His own second coming, but the Father alone does, could it be that Jesus gave up His attribute of omniscience while He was on earth?" And more: "For the same reason, how could the Father and the Son be coequal?" The questions stirred up discussions among the group members.

The verse quoted above, Matthew 24:36, is the answer by the Lord Jesus to His disciples who wanted to know the day of Tribulation and subsequent return of the Lord (see Matt. 24:3). The group discussion concluded that the Lord gave the parable of ten virgins who went out to meet the bridegroom (Matt. 25:1ff); thus the Lord was telling the disciples, and Christians today as well, to be alert, waiting for the day of His second coming, for that day can come anytime. The Lord was also warning us to keep our faith to the end and take heed not to be disturbed by something other than Scripture says, such as end-time prophecies of a Mayan astrological calendar, the Hollywood movie *2012*, or the oracles of Nostradamus.

The group was getting the right messages, but these conclusions are interpretations of the Lord's warnings addressed to His followers. Unfortunately, the study group stopped short of a direct answer to the question, "Why doesn't the Son know the day of His own second coming?"

Another interpretation is that by saying that the Father alone knows the day and time, the Lord was showing the ultimate humility in relation with the Father. It is true so far as humility is concerned, but the question was about omniscience and equality.

John MacArthur has a thorough discussion on the Second Coming.[57] Therefore, I have nothing more to add, except to ask a few questions of my own and try to answer them—a standard approach to Bible study:

- The verse is clear and straightforward. It is not symbolic. The Lord said He did not know. Why shouldn't we accept what He said and not raise the

---

57 John F. MacArthur, *The Second Coming* (Illinois: Crossway Books, 1999).

question? Alternatively, couldn't we find the reason in the Scripture as to why the Lord Jesus did not know?

- Why must we assume that He gave up His omniscience when He said He did not know?—a challenge to the study group discussion.

- Can we find a parallel (or similarity) from a scientific perspective to help reveal the answer, so that it will show another proof that science is a gift of God for us to understand the Scripture better?

The reflections on these questions lead to my answers:

1. Christ does not lie (Titus 1:2), so I believe the Lord Jesus did not know.

2. Contrary to what the question may imply, I believe the Lord has shown His attribute of omniscience even more, by not knowing the day of His return.

Why? In the six-days of Creation, the Scripture says "God saw that it was good" at the end of each day, except the second day (we will talk about this in the next chapter). This means that God *did not know* whether the outcome of His action would please Him or not, before actually seeing His own creation. Does this make God less omniscient? No!

If it would limit His omniscience, it would be because of our misguided definition of omniscience, a matter of our denying God His will to choose. That would place man above God. Doesn't this sound familiar—the story about Lucifer, the fallen angel, who wanted to be above God? In this sense I believe the Lord Jesus would never interfere with the will of the Father (John 6:38).

In the book of Revelation, we are told that the Tribulation will start when Jesus Christ breaks the seven seals of a scroll. It is a book of the end-time prophecies for the future, but Jesus knew everything about it while He was still on earth (Matt. 24); in that sense I believe He did not give up His attribute of omniscience.

The Lord Jesus knew beforehand that He would be the *only one* worthy of breaking the seven seals of the scroll (Revelation 5:5, 9), because according to the Scripture, Jesus said, "All authority in heaven and on earth has been given to me" (Matt. 28:18, NIV). This means Jesus Christ knew that the One who sits in the heavenly throne would give the scroll to Him and no one else. Whenever the One would be ready to give Christ the scroll, He would do the honor of breaking the seals, but He wouldn't know when the scroll would be handed to Him. It is for the One on the throne to decide when. (The Almighty had His will to say that "it was good" in the beginning; He will have His will to say "enough is enough" at the end time.)

So the Lord Jesus said in the Scripture that He wouldn't know the day and hour the tribulation would start. Even Jesus Christ does not interfere with the Father's choice, so who are we to do otherwise? Thus by His testimony of not knowing the day and hour of His second coming, His attribute of omniscience is even more firmly established, because the Lord knew beforehand that He would be the One to open the scroll, and that the tribulation and His second coming would follow after the seals are broken.

I believe the important thing is that even the Lord is alert, waiting for the scroll to be handed to Him. Shouldn't we also be alert and faithfully waiting for the second coming of the Lord?

3. I certainly agree that the Lord Jesus displayed the utmost humility by saying that only the Father knows, but I also believe that He was humble throughout His thirty-three years on earth. The Lord said:

> Truly, truly, I say to you, a slave is not greater than his master, nor is one who is sent greater than the one who sent him. (John 13:16)

This verse tells us that His disciples, whom the Lord was going to send out to mission, couldn't be greater than their master who sent them. Then He said:

> Truly, truly, I say to you, he who receives whomever I send receives Me; and he who receives Me receives Him who sent Me. (John 13:20)

Clearly, the Lord Jesus was saying that He was sent by the Father, and therefore He couldn't be greater than the Father.

So then, returning to the question: "How could we say the Father and the Son are coequal?" it is a good question, but I believe that it stems from the misunderstanding of the meaning of coequal; in fact, we must ask, "Coequal in what?"

We already have described in the previous chapter the analogy of three primary colors. The BGR colors are distinguishable in wavelengths (or frequencies), and we know that a blue photon, which has higher frequency, has more energy than a red photon, but they are *equal* in the sense that they are fundamentally the same electromagnetic waves.

Apostle Paul stated in the epistle that the Lord Jesus, "although being essentially one with God and in the form of God [possessing the fullness of the attributes which make God God], did not think this *equality* with God was a thing to be eagerly grasped or retained" (Phil. 2:6, Amplified; emphasis added). Clearly, it was the Lord's choice to be humble, but the equality comes in the Lord's nature as God. In our human terms, it may be easier to understand if we say, metaphorically, that the Father and the Son are coequal in having the same DNA, not in their titles or their offices.

Another analogy may help seekers see the parallel between the spiritual world and the world of physics.

Let us consider the simplest Bohr's model of a hydrogen atom which consists of an electron (negatively charged) orbiting around a proton (positively charged, making the atom electrically neutral as a whole). Only certain orbits, called quantized energy levels, are allowed.

When the electron is in the lowest orbit, the atom is said to be in the ground energy state. Left alone, a hydrogen atom tends to be in the ground state. When the atom is excited, having absorbed energy from an external source such as a stream of light quanta (photons), the electron will jump to a higher orbit, and the atom is said to be in the first excited state. As more energy is absorbed, the electron jumps to the next even higher orbit, and the atom is said to be in the second excited state, and so on, until the electron escapes from the proton, at which point we call it a free electron.

On the other hand, an electron orbiting at a higher energy level can also make a transition to a lower level, emitting photons in the process. However, the absorption or emission of photons by state transition between two energy states can take place only when the photon has a frequency (v, the Greek letter *nu*) related to the energy *difference* between these two quantized levels (ΔE) by the equation $\Delta E = hv$ (where h is Planck's constant).

Now let us see the parallel in the spiritual world by first listing several verses in the Scripture:

(A) In the beginning God created the heavens and the earth. (Gen. 1:1)

(B) I [the apostle Paul] know a man in Christ who fourteen years ago—whether in the body I do not know, or out of the body I do not know, God knows—such a man was caught up to the third heaven. (2 Cor. 12:2)

(C) For I have come down from heaven, not to do My own will, but the will of Him who sent Me. (John 6:38)

(D) I am the Light of the world. (John 8:12)

Note that in *(A)* the word "heavens" is in plural. In *(B)* the apostle Paul confirmed that the heavens are in multiple levels. Paul's spirit was caught up to the third level (analogically the third excited state) by absorbing a mysterious energy, and eventually he came back down to earth (the ground energy state).

In *(C)*, the Scripture says that Christ came down from heaven, from the throne of glory to this lowly earth. Analogically, the heavenly throne is in the highest energy level, and earth is in the ground state. He referred to Himself (metaphorically) as the light to humankind (John 1:4)—analogically the emission of light accompanied by this energy state transition.

This *downward* transition of atoms from excited state to the ground state in physics can help us perceive the *incarnation* of Christ from spirit to human flesh in the Scripture. On the other hand, the *upward* transition from ground state to an excited state in physics can help us perceive the *resurrection* of Christ by analogy. I believe that Jesus Christ, upon resurrection, was analogically in an excited energy state, for He could appear in the midst of His disciples in an enclosed room. This is something more than an ordinary person in ground energy state could do.

His *ascension* to heaven, back to His throne, is analogous to an upward transition to the highest level, no longer bound by human flesh.

The Father and Christ are coequal in the sense that both are in the highest glorious state receiving worship from all things that they created:

> [Angels, elders, and living creatures were] saying with a loud voice, "Worthy is the Lamb that was slain to receive power and riches and wisdom and might and honor and glory and blessing."
>
> And every created thing which is in heaven and on the earth and under the earth and on the sea, and all things in them, I heard saying, "To Him who sits on the throne, and to the Lamb, be blessing and honor and glory and dominion forever and ever." (Revelation 5:12–13)

They are coequally receiving the worship of all creation. It wouldn't happen if the Lord Jesus were not God, for the first of the Ten Commandments forbids it.

I believe God carried out His creation according to certain rules, and science is the study of those rules. And science turns out to be a tool that can help us perceive the things in the spiritual world by analogy. Thus, science is a gift of God indeed.

9. Science is a Gift of God (IV) —
The day God did not say that it was good

———————— 〜 ————————

> Then God said, "Let there be an expanse in the midst of the waters, and let it separate the waters from the waters."
>
> God made the expanse, and separated the waters which were below the expanse from the waters which were above the expanse; and it was so.
>
> God called the expanse heaven. And there was evening and there was morning, a second day. (Genesis 1:6–8)

Let us start by asking a few questions on the above Scripture first and then meditate:

- What did the writer of the creation narrative see in the vision? Again it had to be a vision, for the writer was not there at the time of creation. And the vision had to be shown by God, because the Scripture tells us something that scientists have observed only in the last couple of centuries.

- Why did God call it *expanse* between waters rather than *emptiness* or *void*, similar to words used in Genesis 1:2? Is there a special meaning here, or is it just a stylistic choice to avoid repetition of words? More important is the question– could it be that the expanse is not exactly empty or void?

- Normal objects (not the dark matter postulated by scientists) are known to attract each other by gravity. However, the Scripture says that God separated cosmic cloud or waters against gravitational force. Does this mean God created antigravity (repulsive force) as well as gravity (attractive force)? Does science confirm this statement?

- Of all the six days of creation narratives, Scripture says, "God saw that it was good," at the end of each day, except this second day. Why?

Now, let us reflect on the above questions with the aid of what we know in twenty–first–century science. If there is a parallel or similarity between the two, Scripture is ahead of science by four thousand years, and the science is the gift of God for us to understand the Bible clearer.

God Did Not Say that It Was Good

On Day 1, God detonated the big bang explosion to create the universe filled with trillions of elementary particles and antiparticles from nothingness. The infant universe was created in less than three seconds. But in the vision of Day 2 the creation process could have taken billions of years: the subatomic particles formed atoms, and atoms formed molecules–first simple and lighter elements such as hydrogen, helium ..., oxygen ...; then heavier elements—silicon, iron, nickel—then complex molecules. The *waters* can mean water molecules (compound molecules of hydrogen and oxygen), and cosmic dust[58] moving like streams of water passing by the writer of Genesis in a vision of the *expanding* universe. The cosmic dust then formed the interstellar clouds from which stars, planets, and galaxies are made. I believe what the writer saw on the second day (one writer's 24-hour viewing session) could be billions of years of creation *in progress.*

---

58 The terminology has no specific application for describing materials found on the planet Earth, other than in the most general sense that all elements with an atomic mass higher than hydrogen are believed to be formed in the cores of stars via stellar nucleosynthesis and supernova nucleosynthesis events. All elements that exist can be indiscriminately considered to be a form of "cosmic dust" (Wikipedia).

The creation *in progress* is unlike the *end result* of the creation of the day such as light, waters, lands, or trees. By *not* saying "God saw that it was good," I believe the Scripture wants us to know that it was a long creation *process* without a result that the writer could discern in the viewing session of Day 2.

If this interpretation is acceptable, not only does every word Scripture says have purpose, but a word that the Scripture *intentionally* omits on purpose has an important implication as well. I cannot help but believe that the Scripture was indeed written by the inspiration of God.

The Expanse

When the Scripture uses the word *expanse* instead of *emptiness* or *void*, could it mean that there is some kind of substance which we do not yet know in the expanse?

- *Newton's Aether (Ether) Model:*

    While sound can only propagate in media such as gas, liquid, or solid, light can propagate from stars in other galaxies to our planet Earth through open space. Thus Isaac Newton postulated (*Opticks*, 1704) that the open space in the universe is not empty but filled with an invisible medium, called the *aether*, to support the propagation of light (Newton's luminiferous aether).

Debates on the existence of aether have never ceased, since the day Isaac Newton postulated it. While many scientists dismissed the hypothesis of aether, we see its revival in recent years. Eric Baird and many others believe that Newton's *modified aether model* can be considered as an early attempt at a curved-space model of gravity,[59] similar to Einstein's warped space.

- *String Theory Model:*

  Since 1969, in an attempt to reconcile quantum mechanics and general field theory, some theoretical physicists have postulated that elementary particles are not particles but strings vibrating at different resonant frequencies. The model is still in development, and there is no way scientists can prove its existence *experimentally* with *present–day* technology. They are still a long way from a convincing explanation of gravitational force using string theory. If space is filled with invisible and infinitesimally small strings, could it be the quantum-mechanical

---

59 Eric Baird, *Newton's Aether Model*, (http://arxiv.org/ftp/physics/papers/0011/0011003.pdf)

counterpart of Newton's aether model or the dual property of aether? It seems that Newton's initial aether postulation cannot be completely ignored.

- *Dark Energy and Dark Matter Model:*

  Several mysterious phenomena in the universe have led the astrophysicists and particle physicists to postulate the existence of energy and matter in the universe which is invisible to humans. The scientists came to this conclusion as a result of the following observations: (1) The mass distribution of the visible universe is extremely anisotropic (non-uniform), as evidenced by the clusters of galaxies. If the universe was created from one point of singularity, the mass distribution of the universe had to be isotropic (homogeneous and no preferred direction). However, *assuming the existence* of dark matter means that the visible and invisible mass combined together in the universe restores the possibility that the overall distribution is isotropic.[60]

---

60 Could it be that the invisible 95 percent of the universe is isotropic and the visible 5 percent is the *special* handwork of God, the Almighty (Ps. 19:1)?

(2) As recently as 1998, scientists observed that the universe is expanding at an *accelerating* rate. If we just consider the big bang explosion, the force causing the expansion should decrease as the volume of the universe increases. The observed acceleration is a mystery and must be caused by something else. Scientists have attributed it to the existence of dark energy and matter that accelerate the expansion.

(3) Observation shows that stars revolving around the center of galaxies at a constant speed over a large range of distances from the center of the galaxy. Thus the stars are revolving much faster than would be expected by Newtonian mechanics. (Namely, the rotation rates of spiral galaxies do not exhibit the same pattern of decreasing orbital velocity with increasing distance from the center of mass observed in the Solar System.) Astronomers call this phenomenon the "flattening of galaxies' rotation curves", and scientists hypothetically explain this phenomenon by Modified Newtonian Dynamics or by the existence of dark matters. [61]

---

61 Wikipedia, http://en.wikipedia.org/wiki/Galaxy_rotation_curve; http://en.wikipedia.org/wiki/MOND

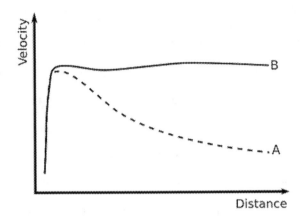

Figure 3: Flattening of galaxies' rotation curves
Expected (A) and observed (B) star velocities as a
function of distance from the galactic center

To explain cosmic phenomena, hundreds of different models are proposed and debated by scientists. Astrophysicists are in favor of the MACHO model (MAssive Compact Halo Objects), in which they believe the dark matter is composed of baryonic particles. The baryonic is defined as the same type of elementary particles as exist in the visible part of the universe. On the other hand, the high-energy particle physicists are in favor of the WIMPs model (Weakly Interacting Massive Particles), in which they believe the dark matter is composed of non–baryonic particles. The non-baryonic is defined as a new type of elementary particles not yet detected by direct observation.[62]

---

62 Chris Miller, *Cosmic Hide and Seek: The Search for the Missing Mass,* http://www.eclipse.net/~cmmiller/DM/ Kim Griest, *The Nature of the Dark Matter,* Physics Department, UC, San Diego, http://web.mit.edu/redingtn/ www/netadv/specr/012/012.html; see also many articles in Wikipedia.

Whether it is aether, dark matter, or even something else, the open space does not seem to be empty or void—as the inside of an inflating balloon is not empty. Thus I believe it was why the writer of Genesis did not use the word *empty* or *void* on Day 2. If this is true, the Bible has already implied that the *expanse* is not nothingness.

At present, two models are leading contenders to explain the expanding universe: quintessence and the cosmological constant. Both models conclude that the dark energy must have negative pressure shown by the stress-energy tensor of field theory. Thus, when the Scripture says that *God made the expanse, and separated the waters which were below the expanse from the waters which were above the expanse* (against gravitational force), it is supported by science.

If you look into what scientists have proposed, you will find so many assumptions, hypotheses, and postulations are made in each model that some are more metaphysics[63] than physics. Furthermore, for each model proposed by someone, you will find that hundreds of other scientists *modify* it to generate many more new models, and additional hundreds *oppose* and dismiss the model(s). I suggest that those atheists and skeptics who give credit to science for everything and deny the existence of the Creator should read about all the models of the universe found

---

63 A division of philosophy that is concerned with the fundamental nature of reality and being and that includes ontology, cosmology, and often epistemology (merriam-webster.com).

in books, papers, Wikipedia, and NASA reports. They will find that one needs at least as much faith to believe in science as to believe in the Bible.

Let us propose a model that can explain observed phenomena and may reconcile many models as well as interpret what the writer of Genesis might have seen in the vision. This simple model uses the most basic high school science, instead of the multidimensional stress–energy tensors of field theory.

Let's try the idea of *special* relativity in everyday language first and then this metaphysical model.

Special Relativity

Assume you are holding a candle, and for the sake of argument say the candle is originally six inches long and it would take six hours to burn out (burning one inch per hour at a constant rate). I am holding a movie camera, and when you light up the candle, I start filming the candle. As one feature of the camera, a time marker records the passing seconds. When the time marker says that it is at the end of the sixth hour, we will see that the candle is burning down to nothing. In this case, there is no relative motion between the candle and the camera. That is, the relative velocity (V) between the two objects, the candle and the camera, is zero, V=0.

Now let us consider three different cases. In each scenario, I am riding on a fictitious high-speed spaceship leaving you and the candle at a constant speed V, and taking the picture of the candle with my camera. The moment you light up the candle, I turn on my camera and leave the earth.

These three cases are:

(1) V < c, the spaceship leaves you at a constant speed that is less than the speed of light c.

(2) V = c, the spaceship leaves you at the speed of light.

(3) V > c, the spaceship leaves you at a speed greater than the speed of light. (Objects cannot travel faster than the speed of light, according to Einstein's special theory of relativity, but assume for the moment that this hypothetical ship can.)

Let us see the video screen on my camera in the spaceship.

In case (1), V < c, for the sake of argument, let us assume my spaceship is traveling at *one-half* the speed of light. On *Earth*, you see the candle burned out completely at the end of six hours, but *on the spaceship* the screen of my camera shows that the image of the candle still has 0.804 inches left and is burning. And by the time my screen shows the totally burned-out candle, the time marker shows 6 hours and 55 minutes. This is because the *scene* (or *image*) of the burned-out candle has to take another 55 minutes to catch up with my camera to get into the video screen. (Calculation is based on Lorenz factor in relativity theory.)

In case (2), V = c, my spaceship is traveling at the speed of light. The ship left the earth when the candle was of the original length. When on earth the candle has already burned out to nothing, the image on the video camera still shows the original length—the same original scene as when the ship left earth. This is because the camera is traveling at the same speed as light from the original scene is traveling. No matter how far it goes, even if it takes an infinite flight time, the video will still show the same image of you and the candle. This case creates a barrier beyond which our daily physics cease to be applicable.

In case (3), V > c, my camera is traveling at a speed greater than the speed of light. Thus the image of you and the candle can never catch up with my camera, and as a result nothing will show up on the video screen. Though you and the candle exist on earth, I and the camera cannot see you, just as if you did not exist.

Up to here, the point I would like to make is this: though there are things we do not see, that does not necessarily mean they do not exist. When the *relative* speed of a star of a distant galaxy with the observer on earth exceeds the speed of light in the expanding universe, the red-shift theoretically will shift beyond infrared, making the spectral line undetectable with a spectrophotometer (or spectrometer); it will have shifted into the invisible *microwave* range of the radiation spectrum.

(Note: two objects traveling in opposite directions, each at less than light speed can make their *relative* speed exceed light speed, and it is not necessary that the absolute speed of one object has to exceed the light speed. If this is true, we might have to reconsider the problem of isotropy, or lack of it, in counting the distribution of mass in the universe, because the stars are there but we cannot detect them.)

An Intuitive Metaphysical Model

Now let us propose an intuitive metaphysical model. God detonated the big bang, and the enormous explosion tore up the nothingness into trillions of elementary particles and antiparticles which formed matter and antimatter. In order to prevent these from annihilating each other and a return of the nothingness, God spatially separated these two groups of particles by setting everything into motion—making them, from subatomic particles to cosmic bodies, spin around their own axes and at the same time revolve around one another. There has to be a supernatural Being who sets everything into motion (as Sir Isaac Newton believed).

Our Milky Way happens to be one of the normal matter–dominated (electron-dominated) galaxies, and somewhere in the universe, God is keeping antimatter-dominated (positron-dominated) galaxies away so as to prevent the two types of galaxies from mutual annihilation. (Note: the naming of matter and antimatter is arbitrary. One may call our electron-dominated galaxy antimatter, and then the other kind would be normal matter.)

At the moment of the big bang explosion, all elementary particles traveled outward from the point of singularity at all *possible speeds.*

Definition: V_J particles and V_R particles

As the heat accompanying the big bang explosion cooled down, God set a threshold speed V_T and grouped all particles into two groups relative to the threshold. Namely, the particles traveling or *spinning* at speed less than the threshold $V < V_T$ in one region, let's call it region "R" (meaning real, and visible to humans), and the particles traveling or spinning at speed greater than the threshold $V > V_T$ in another region, let's call it region "J" (meaning invisible region, which is considered to be imaginary to humans, and the letter J is commonly used to represent the imaginary part of a complex number, because the letter "I" has been exclusively used to designate electrical current in engineering). The particles in region R we shall call V_R particles, and those in region J, V_J particles.

These two regions are separated by a momentum (energy) barrier $V = V_T$. While the V_R particles are visible, the V_J particles are invisible by the argument presented in the above section. V_J particles, which occupy 95 percent of the universe, are invisible—traveling or *spinning* at speeds faster than the threshold.

This threshold value V_T *happens* to be equal to the speed of light c in *vacuum.*

$V_T = c = 1/ (\varepsilon_0\mu_0)^{1/2}$, where ε_0 is the permittivity and μ_0 is the permeability of vacuum, according to Maxwell's electromagnetic wave equations.[64]

Postulation 1: Assuming the Lorenz factor (γ) is valid in region J as in region R,

$$\gamma_R = 1/ (1-V_R^2/V_T^2)^{1/2} \text{ for } V_R < V_T$$
$$\gamma_J = 1/ (1- V_J^2/ V_T^2)^{1/2} = - J/ (V_J^2/ V_T^2 - 1)^{1/2} \text{ for } V_J > V_T$$
and $J^2 = -1$

Postulation 2: Assuming application of special relativity is valid for both regions,

$$m_R = m_0\, \gamma_R \text{ and } m_J = m_0\, \gamma_J$$

where m_0 is the stationary mass, then

Mass m_R in region R is a *real* number,

Mass m_J in region J is an *imaginary* number

Thus, m_J, represented by an imaginary number, is *invisible* mass to humans.

---

64 In Maxwell's time, it was not yet known that the universe is finite and expanding at an *accelerating* rate and that dark energy and dark matter may exist in the space occupied by what scientists at that time called "vacuum". When these factors are considered, the permeability and permittivity of vacuum and therefore, the constant speed of light in *vacuum*, may have to be redefined. Thus we use the term Threshold Speed V_T.

Light speed can be slowed down at extreme low temperature and vacuum, from 186,282 miles *a second* to 38 miles *an hour*, as demonstrated by Harvard University physicists. http://www.news.harvard.edu/gazette/1999/02.18/light.html

Postulation 3: Assuming Newton's universal law of gravity is valid in both regions,

i.e., $\quad F = G \, m_1 \, m_2 \, / \, r^2$

where F is gravitational force; G is the constant of gravity; m_1, m_2 are masses of two objects and r is the distance separating them.

Then force of gravity between two objects in region R is *positive* (the product of two positive real numbers is positive), a force of attraction. And the gravitational force between two objects in region **J** is *negative* (the product of two negative imaginary numbers is a negative real number), a force of repulsion. (This is similar to the negative pressure in the model of stress-energy tensor in field theory.)

To this point, the present model is similar to the WIMPs (Weakly Interacting Massive Particles) model in the sense that V_J particles and V_R particles cannot interact strongly, for the force between the two is an imaginary number by Newton's universal law of gravity (product of a real number and a negative imaginary number is a negative imaginary number). Thus the baryonic photons from other galaxies can be observed or detected from earth and not scattered by non-baryonic particles. The V_J particles are *massive* in the sense that they are spinning faster than the threshold speed.

Again the Scripture is scientifically sound as God says, "Let there be an expanse between the waters to separate water from water."

The Orbiting Speed at the Edge of a Galaxy

At the boundary of the two regions where the invisible region J surrounds the visible region R, such as our visible Milky Way galaxy for example, the following can happen by the above postulations.

- Two regions are separated by a *momentum barrier* at which the value of the Lorenz factor is infinite $\gamma = \infty$, where $V = V_T$.

- When the speed of particles exceeds the threshold $V_J > V_T$, the *magnitude* of γ_J is no longer infinite, $|\gamma_J| < \infty$. In fact, the *magnitude* of the Lorenz factor $|\gamma_J|$ decreases as V_J increases (two vertical bars represent absolute value or magnitude).

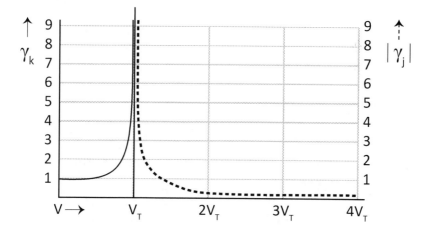

Figure 4: Lorenz Factor vs. speed of particles in both regions
(Solid line for R region, and dotted line for J region)

- At the edge of a galaxy, where the J region surrounds the R region, the gravitational repulsion of the J region exerts force on the momentum barrier to *confine* the R region. Without the J region, the edge of a galaxy would have orbited around the center of galaxy at a slower speed. But the force exerted by the J region on the boundary makes the *apparent* force of gravitational attraction at the edge from the center of the galaxy *stronger*—(i.e., the apparent force on the edge toward center = actual attractive force from the center + additional force exerted toward the center by the external repulsive force due to the J region.)—and that makes objects at the edge of a galaxy orbit around its center at the same rate as objects closer to the center, i.e., independent of their distance from the center of the galaxy, as *observed* by the astronomers. (As shown in Figure 3: Flattening of galaxies' rotation curves.)

Postulation 4: *Flow of particles*: At the boundary of the two regions, V_J particles can get through the momentum barrier from J to R region by *quantum tunneling*. However, tunneling through the barrier can occur only under a condition where the Lorenz factors of the particles in the two regions have the same magnitude $|\gamma_J| = \gamma_R$ but different speeds because $V_J \gg V_T \gg V_R$.[65]

The V_J particles making the transition from J region to R region will *lose spin speed*; and release energy, exotic particles, and photons; and become less energetic V_J particles[66] ($V_J \gg V_T \gg V_R$ in J region, becomes $V_J > V_T \gg V_R$ in R region). Such an assumption enables us to harmonize the MACHO model and the WIMPs model. The visible photon released at the boundary may appear as the halo phenomenon as in MACHO model and observed by astronomers.

Postulation 5: *Center of galaxies:* In order to maintain the flow of V_J particles in equilibrium, there must be a mechanism that makes V_J particles which got into the R region return to the J region. This is where the center of the galaxy comes into play. The center of a galaxy spins so fast that it accelerates the V_J particles nearby. These particles gain momentum (speed) so much (restore the speed V_J before they entered the R region) that they are spit out of the galaxy and back into the J region. The spit-out amount makes room (analogous to holes for electrons to flow in semiconductors) for replenishing the V_J particles which got into the R region from the edge of the galaxy. Thus a current

---

65 It is analogous to electrons tunneling through the energy barrier in a semiconductor tunneling device, when the conduction band of one side of a junction and the valence band of the other side are aligned at the same energy level.

66 Analogously, electrons in the conduction band have higher mobility than when they are in the valence band.

flow of V_J particles is maintained – flowing from edge of the galaxy into the R region by tunneling, continue toward the center of galaxy and then out of the galaxy from its center and back to invisible J region (as in Figure 5). Since the V_J particles are by definition invisible (for $V_J \gg V_T$), the center of the galaxy is dark. (People call it a black hole. One may call it to have massive mass, momentum, kinetic energy and spin speed.) Consequently the stream of V_J particles shoots out from the plane of the revolving galaxy and returns to the invisible J-region.

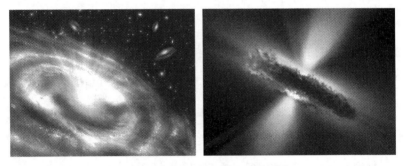

Figure 5a: Images from NASA

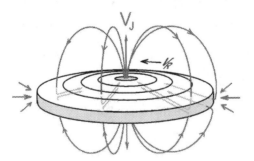

Figure 5b: Sketch of a proposed model where revolving direction of the visible galaxy is on horizontal plane, and the flow directions of invisible V_J particles are on both horizontal and vertical planes.

If the rate at which V_J particles get into the R region by tunneling through the momentum barrier and the rate at which the V_J particles are recovered from the center of galaxy are *not* equal, the galaxy will either collapse or disintegrate. God controls the life of a galaxy as He controls the life of a person.

This model postulates that the spinning of a galaxy (normal V_R particles) together with the flow of V_J particles (vertical to the plane of galaxy disk) combined *generate* gravitational field. This is analogous to circulating electric charges generate magnetic flux and together they radiate electromagnetic fields. (Note: However, *postulation* of this V_R-V_J flow is different from electromagnetic field in that the magnetic field forms magnetic dipole.)

Postulation 6: Two nearby galaxies attract each other; but the V_J particles surrounding each of them restrain the two from collision (the same repulsive force by which God separated the waters above and the waters below the expanse as the Bible says). However, if the equilibrium of the V_J particle flow of either one of the galaxies is destroyed for any reason, two galaxies may collide and merge into one (for the repulsive force becomes weaker than the attractive force). The case of such collision (or merging) of galaxies has been observed by astronomers.

Different Disciplines of Sciences Correlate

In this model, we assumed the validity of Lorenz factor for $V > V_T$, where the mass of an object in the J region is a quantity expressible only in imaginary numbers. Although some physicists may dismiss the validity of imaginary numbers in our normal physics, complex numbers have long been extensively applied in solving practical problems by electrical engineers and some physicists, since the days of the great electrical engineer Charles Proteus Steinmetz (April 9, 1865- October 23, 1923).

In electrical engineering, the exchange of energy between capacitor and inductor in a tank circuit; between electrical field and magnetic field, is a familiar phenomenon. The fact that an electron can tunnel through an energy barrier is familiar to electrical engineers in semiconductor technology and to solid-state physicists.

It seems that analogies can be applied from different fields of study, such as engineering, classical physics (for large-scale objects), quantum physics (for subatomic particles), to astrophysics. After all, all things are created by the one Almighty with His rules governing the universe and everything in it. The point is this: just as we can understand a passage of Scripture better by correlating it with other passages of the Bible, one may be able to understand the mysteries of the universe better by correlating all branches of sciences, technologies, and even the Scripture.

Beloved readers, I am sure God will allow us to find more and more mysteries of universe as technology progresses to detect them. For each discovery, I am equally certain that new models will mushroom along the way. Thus, by no means am I claiming that the rudimentary model outlined here can explain all the mysteries of the universe. Rather, I am pointing out that we can make all the models we want—even I, a man of frail and feeble mind—but the mysteries of the universe are too complex for humans to handle. We cannot see or touch the invisible 95 percent of the universe. No matter how many partial differential equations are defined the parameters and coefficients are neither constant nor necessarily linear, so I believe.

Just for example, the permittivity and permeability of dark matter are unknown. Problems become even more complex when we note that the universe is expanding with *acceleration* instead of constant speed. As the universe expands, permittivity and permeability are most likely functions of time, space, mass density, gravity gradient, intensity of electric and magnetic fields, and so on and on.

It has been reported that at an extremely super-low temperature and super-vacuum in controlled laboratory condition, a light beam has been engineered to slow down from 186,282 miles *a second* to 38 miles *an hour*, by Harvard University physicists.[67] We do not know the conditions of outer space between galaxies, not to mention between normal matter galaxies and antimatter galaxies.

If light speed can slow down in part of the universe, scientists' estimates of the size or the lifespan of the universe become

---

67 The Harvard University Gazette, see http://www.news. harvard.edu/gazette/1999/02.18/light.html

more uncertain. *Again I say we need as much faith to believe in science as in the Bible.*

Furthermore, we do not even know the initial conditions and boundary values of the universe, of which 95 percent is invisible and untouchable, to solve those equations properly.

We can keep on generating one model after another, but we are like the six blind men touching different parts of a giant elephant and reporting back different perceptions of what they think they know about the elephant. I do honor the values of scientific researches (in fact, I consider myself a research engineer), but the most concise and precise explanation of all is still the Scripture in the Holy Bible: In the beginning God created the heavens and the earth, and He showed it to the writer of Genesis in a vision, so I believe.

Life on Other Planets:

Finally, the Bible mentions the solar system on the fourth day. Thus, the vision of the creation process, in which God separating the waters above from the waters below on the second day and gathering waters to show land on the third day, appears to be meant for cosmic bodies in general.

Therefore, if waters and living organisms are found on planets other than planet Earth, it would only confirm that the sequential description of the creation in the Bible is accurate.

10. Science and Religion Will Converge into Faith in God

—————————— ❧ ——————————

Stephen Hawking Says God Did Not Create the Universe:

What Do You Think?

"World News" Wants to Know What You Think: Do You Agree or Disagree?

This poll is found in the September 2, 2010, ABC World News online.[68] It recorded the conversation between the renowned theoretical physicist Stephen Hawking and Diane Sawyer, the anchorwoman of the program.

The World News is asking whether the viewer agrees. My response is too long for a simple yes–or–no opinion poll, so here is what I think.

———————

68 http://abcnews.go.com/WN/Technology/stephen-hawking-religion-science-win/story?id=10830164.

Stephen Hawking says that he does not believe in a personal god. Albert Einstein said something similar fifteen months before his death, *only it is in a different context.*[69] Einstein was not convinced by Eric Gutkind that the Jews were the chosen people favored by the God of the Bible and replied that such a belief would be a weak nation's childish superstition. But the facts indicate that: (1) One of the leading experts on Einstein, John Brooke of Oxford University, said that Einstein became angry when his views were appropriated by evangelists for atheism. So he was not an atheist. (2) Einstein believed in an illimitable superior spirit. And he said, "Science without religion is lame, religion without science is blind." So he did not dismiss religion (See both quotations in Chapter 6). (3) Atheists, who would say anything to claim Einstein as their own, said they believe in the last word as truth of a person's thought when a person is near the end of his or her life. This is an unfounded conjecture; it can be easily taken as exactly the opposite in many cases.

In Einstein's case, we must keep in mind that the letter was a private communication; we do not know the circumstances in which the debate between Einstein and Gutkind started or continued. It is possible that Einstein couldn't agree about certain parts of organized religion, which might have caused him to decline an invitation to be the state of Israel's second president. We

---

69 http://www.guardian.co.uk/science/2008/may/12/ peopleinscience.religion; http://www.digitaljournal. com/article/254649; http://www.digitaljournal.com/ article/254649#ixzz13olishLD

cannot judge what Einstein meant, by not knowing (1) the content of the Israeli government's offer; (2) his *previous* communication or argument with Eric Gutkind prior to this well-hyped letter; (3) if there was another private communication after this letter, which cannot be hyped to draw a high auction price.

Now, let us turn to the interview between Diane Sawyer and Stephen Hawking. The conversation is in public. To begin, we respect Hawking as a great thinker and acknowledge his contribution to the advancement of science in astrophysics, but he is not God. I suggest that atheists, who claim Einstein or Hawking as one of their own, should Google-search with key words "Einstein wrong." His famous theory of relativity says that one of a pair of twins traveling in outer space at high speed will be younger than his twin on earth—an assertion that turns out to be wrong. An experimental fact reported by NASA shows astronauts age faster in space than people on earth.[70] I wouldn't come out and say, "Einstein wrong", but when he used twins to illustrate his theory of relativity, he was only concerned with the idea of relativity as it pertained to *theoretical* physics; he had not taken into consideration knowledge from other branches of science, such as biology, physiology, etc. Could Hawking be making a similar mistake? Hawking had made mistake before. His 30 years of debate with Stanford University professor Leonard Susskind and Nobel laureate Gerard t'Hooft

---

70 NASA report online http://science.nasa.gov/science-news/
    science-at-nasa/2006/22mar_telomeres/

(1999 Physics) on the Hawking Paradox is well known in the scientific community.

However, we must accept mistakes in modeling and realize that modifying theories to conform to experimental observations are a necessary part of the process of scientific research and advancement. Thus I say, it takes faith to believe in science as well.

Let us reproduce the following excerpt from the interview for the convenience of reference.

> "What could define God [is thinking of God] as the embodiment of the laws of nature. However, this is not what most people would think of that [sic] God," Hawking told Sawyer. "They made a human-like being with whom one can have a personal relationship. When you look at the vast size of the universe and how insignificant an accidental human life is in it, that seems most impossible."
>
> When Sawyer asked if there was a way to reconcile religion and science, Hawking said, "There is a fundamental difference between religion, which is based on authority, [and] science, which is based on observation and reason. Science will win because it works."

God and the Laws of Nature

If I understand the above statement correctly, Hawking believes in a god, but the god he believes in is not the God in the Bible. He defines his god to be the embodiment of the laws of nature, and he also believes that the existence of human life in the vast universe is accidental.

On the other hand, we Christians believe that our God is not the embodiment of the laws of nature. *It is God who sets the laws that rule nature.* Man did not make a humanlike God. The Scripture clearly says that God is a Spirit, and He made man in His image. It is obvious that Hawking has misunderstood the meaning of "the image of God."

The fundamental difference is that we believe that God made man to have body, mind, and spirit, and Hawking is talking only about the lifeless physical body with physics, which is only one discipline of sciences.

The following illustrations may help clarify my statement.

Difference between Religion and Science

The difference defined by Hawking is an oversimplified view. His view of science is referring to the observation of phenomena of *lifeless* objects and also the scientists' effort to quantitatively study the cause and effect of these physical phenomena.

For example, a legend says: An apple fell from a tree, and Isaac Newton *observed* the phenomenon and concluded the *cause* was due to the attracting force between the earth and the apple, and the *effect* of the force was that the apple fell to the ground. Newton further quantified the magnitude of the force of gravity, the acceleration and the speed of the falling apple. This quantitative study is physics.

Albert Einstein said, "Falling in love has nothing to do with gravity." Although this remark had a humorous intent, there is a truth to it. Falling apples can be quantitatively analyzed by physics and math, but falling in love cannot, for an apple is a visible mass, while love is an invisible emotion of living human beings which cannot be quantified or represented by partial differential equations.

The study of mind is beyond the scope of physics, and I believe Einstein's comment acknowledges it. Besides the body, human mind and emotions such as love, hate, joy, sorrow, peace, and anxiety are feelings. Spirit is one level even higher than emotion, and all three are dealt with in religion.

Contrary to Hawking's belief, we hold the following positions:

- Two fundamentally different branches of study cannot compete, thus there is no such thing as which one wins or which one loses.

- Study of religion requires observation and reasoning just as science does.

- There are areas in which religion works and science does not.

Let us explain our disagreement with illustrations:

God Cannot Be an Embodiment of the Laws of Nature

To preserve rare paintings and artifacts in places such as museums, the temperature, air flow, and humidity must be carefully controlled. Engineers design sensors to measure the values of these atmospheric parameters and send these values into controlling devices. These devices are embedded with integrated circuits such as analog to digital converters that sample and digitize the signals. The signals are then sent to digital comparators to compare the room atmospheric parameters A and the desired parameters B. The output of the comparator can be $A > B$, $A = B$, or $A < B$.

Taking temperature for example, when $A = B$ the room temperature is at the desired value and nothing needs to be done. If $A > B$, the output signal of the comparator activates cooling element to cool the room. If $A < B$, the comparator signal activates heating element until the condition $A = B$ is reached,[71] and similarly for air flow and humidity to maintain the room atmosphere stable and optimum for the artifacts. The control system is synthesized with AND, OR, NOR circuits and their derivatives such as NAND or XOR

---

71 This is a simple explanation to spare readers from servomechanisms, feedback loop control systems, adaptive control systems etc.

circuits, which are operated according to the Boolean rules which we discussed in chapter 6.

We can learn from this illustration the following:

- $A > B$, $A=B$, and $A<B$ can be respectively represented by the difference of the two values: $(A-B)$ = a positive number, $(A-B)$ = zero and $(A-B)$ = a negative number. Thus, we can sample just one difference signal in infinitesimal increment, in other words sampling it at an infinite frequency for digitization[72]. Only humans have the concept of zero (0), positive (+), negative (-), infinitesimal increment (ε) and infinity (∞) in number systems. Based on these concepts, Sir Isaac Newton and Gottfried Leibniz, independently invented differential and integral calculus. And in the digital technology Boolean algebra was developed from the basic Boolean rules (see chapter 6).

- It would be absurd to say, that George Boole, Isaac Newton or Gottfried Leibniz are the embodiments of truth tables, and calculus. Similarly, God who set the rules to create, run, and sustain the universe cannot be defined as the embodiment of the laws of nature.

---

72 Practically, we sample analog signal at an optimum rate called Nyquist rate, discovered by a Swedish-American engineer Harry Nyquist.

- Just as designing the atmosphere control system, God designed the environment so that the planet Earth is suitable for living organisms to sustain life (as well as any other similar planets, if they exist).

- Just as a man likes to preserve rare artifacts that are precious to him, humankind is a precious creation to God. (We will take this up again later.)

- The system can be designed to be self-containing. Human engineers can design a self-organizing system or adaptive control system that can be developed into artificial intelligence systems. Why can't God design a much more sophisticated system? Of course, He can.

- Why can humans do all this? Because humanity was created in God's image; so we believe.

The Universe Cannot Create Itself

Hawking says that God is not needed to create the universe. Let's share our opposing view with illustration. Modern technologies have enabled us to install an automatic parallel parking system in high-end vehicles. The car can carry out parallel parking by itself, without intervention of the driver. But the fact is that a microcomputer is embedded in the system to measure the relative position and the angle of the car with respect to the street curb with sensors. The system further computes the speed and the distance the car ought to move back and forth and automatically steers the wheel accordingly to carry out the parallel parking.

The hardware and software system will never just happen to be in the car by spontaneous appearance. In human terms, research engineers must first invent, design, and implement a prototype system for feasibility testing. When the system works, development engineers refine the system for reliability, manufacturability, and cost effectiveness. Then production engineers develop tools for quality assurance test and cost effective methods to replace damaged components, etc. Only then is the system put into mass production. When the user simply switches on the system and the car does the parallel parking, the driver cannot begin to imagine how many man-hours went into the research-development-production processes. It is wishful thinking or even childish to think that the system is there without any human intervention. The first system exists by having been created, and the system that goes into every car is a copy.

Let me say it again: God *created* Adam from the dust, and the descendants of Adam and Eve appeared through *reproduction*. The genesis of the universe by big bang is creation; the birth and death of stars and galaxies are ongoing processes of reproduction of the originally created material.

To those who believe that the universe was created spontaneously by quantum fluctuation, allow me to remind them that fluctuation can take place only inside the universe where fundamental particles and dark energy have already been made by big bang creation. Therefore matter that comes into being by quantum fluctuation is a result of reproduction, not creation. I do not believe quantum fluctuation can take place outside the expanding universe, where space-time has not yet reached and the laws of our physics do not apply.

Reproduction, which may seem not to involve intervention by God, is in effect the regeneration of the embedded system that works without an engineer's direct intervention, but the reproduced machines work only by the inventor's design (analogous to God's creation) and rules programmed into the system (corresponding to the so-called laws of nature).

One more important issue: when does the chief architect (God) of the creation intervene? The chief architect of the system will intervene (Tribulation and Judgment) when the system is abused by the owner (those who sin against God) or when the system (His creation) is sabotaged (by evils, antichrist, and Satan).

Personal Relationship of God with Man

Hawking advances the notion that it is impossible for God to have personal relationships with us, in view of the fact that the universe is so vast in size and people are so insignificantly small.

However, his argument can go the other way. Just because God is capable of creating such a vast universe, keeping personal relationship with each and every person on this tiny earth is an easy task for Him.

Let us reflect on this with an illustration.

You have heard that computer scientists have developed an artificial intelligence system so that a computer can play a chess match with a human opponent. (IBM Deep Blue, a chess-playing computer, won a six-game match by two to one with three draws against world champion Garry Kasparove on May 11, 1997) They developed software architecture, algorithms, and an intelligent database that stores all the rules governing chess games; all possible relative positions the pieces can occupy; all possible moves that the computer might make in response to a given move of its opponent.

For each move of either side, the computer constantly monitors and analyzes the position and calculates ahead to determine the next step the computer should undertake. The computer scientist keeps in mind that his design would take good care of each chess piece (personal relationship) in the system for the good of the entire game (the universe).

What is the point? I believe *God created the universe and everything in it, and through what we see in this world, God reveals Himself to us so that we may know Him and His work better.* The computer scientist has encoded the rules embedded in the chess game to control the moves of all the pieces in any possible position, to sustain their existence throughout the game. This entails a direct involvement in the role and success of each piece as well as the progress and outcome of the entire game. Just so, by analogy, God has designed the rules (what we call the laws of nature) for creating and controlling everything in the universe, from subatomic particles to the galaxies, for the good of His creation. In His design, God takes a direct interest and potentially has a personal relationship with each creature as well as the entire cosmos.

You've Got Mail

Atheists and agnostics may say that there are only sixty-four locations on the chessboard and two sets of sixteen chess pieces. How could one compare the vast universe with it? It is a very good question! But it is not the problem of accessibility to the entire population of humans on earth. Today, the human population on planet earth is 6,874,300,000. Its binary number is 11010001100100101111100 in a computer-readable form. It is only a 23-bit word. However, even with current technology, human engineers have already made 32-bit, 64-bit, and even 128-bit special purpose machines. Even this 32-bit or 64-bit word can be used to store and retrieve data on each individual in the entire world population. One illustration is that each and every person in the entire world can own an Internet address, and the network can handle it. Another example is the smart meters that gas and electricity companies install in their customers' homes.

The company can read meters remotely without sending people to each house.

Anyone who has a computer connected to the Internet has had the experience of receiving a notice that urges the user to update software from an operating system company such as Microsoft or a computer security company such as McAfee. These companies can access all computers that are linked to the servers in the network. However, it is up to you to decide whether or not you wish to download the package (the software or message).

Precisely because God can create such a vast universe in the first place, keeping personal interest and communication with each and every individual on this *tiny* planet Earth is not a difficult matter for the Almighty. So long as our personal computer is connected to the Internet and we are willing to download the message or package, a relationship between my personal computer and the central computer can be established. By the same token, so long as our God-given soul (the spirit in us) is connected to His Spirit, He will let us know His will.

However, there is one condition: we have to be *willing* to listen to His will (download His message), and we can offer our worship, praise and prayers to Him too (analogous to uploading our messages). On the other hand, if we shut our spiritual eyes, it is analogous to shutting down our connection to the Internet (denying God), and as a consequence no message would reach us. Jesus said, "I am the vine, you are the branches; he who abides in Me and I in him, he bears much fruit, for apart from Me you can do nothing" (John 15:5).

Beloved readers, how would you feel if you use Skype on your computer wanting to talk and see your loved ones anywhere in the world, so as to show your loving concern, and your loved ones just refuse to talk to you by disconnecting their computers from the Internet?

If you can appreciate the feeling, please go connect your spirit with your heavenly Father, who loves you through Jesus Christ. Thus, I believe that science and technology are gifts from God to help us understand Him and His work better. Again studies of mind and spirit are beyond the scope of physics, which studies only the body.

Now let us continue to the next paragraph of the interview:

> When Sawyer asked if there was a way to reconcile religion and science, Hawking said, "There is a fundamental difference between religion, which is based on authority, [and] science, which is based on observation and reason. Science will win because it works."

Hawking seems to think that

(1) Science is based on observation and reason (while religion is not—implied).

- The fact is that Bible study requires observation, interpretation, and application. These are the essentials taught by any books on how to study the Bible, and this book is no exception.

(2) Science will win because it works (while religion will lose, because it does not work—implied).

- The fact is that the science Hawking deals with is only related to the first few verses of the Bible, and the rest is beyond the scope of physics. There are many domains of study in which religion works and science does not. We will give examples later.

(3) There is no way religion and science can be reconciled.

- On the contrary, all disciplines of study are gifts from God, and not only can they be reconciled, they are in fact complementary to each other in order that humanity may know God and His work better.

Let's elaborate on the above statements.

Where the Bible Works, Science Cannot

About 630 years before the birth of Christ, *when a woman was treated as a man's possession rather than an individual human being*, God told the nation of Israel through the prophet Jeremiah,

> How long will you waver and hesitate [to return],
> O you backsliding daughter? For the Lord has
> created a new thing in the land [of Israel]: a
> female shall compass (woo, win, and protect) a
> man. (Jeremiah 31:22, Amplified Bible)

Bible scholars explain that this passage was prophesying that God was going to forgive the nation of Israel, call the people back to the Promised Land from 2,000 years of exile, and rebuild the nation. Some 2,600 years later, the prophecy was fulfilled. The nation of Israel was reborn on May 14, 1948.

What the Bible scholars have not mentioned in their commentaries is that two of the twenty-four who signed the Israeli declaration of independence were women, and one of the two, Golda Meir, subsequently became the first woman prime minister of Israel in 1969. Most amazingly, the prophecy was even literally realized.[73] Can this be quantitatively analyzed by physics or math? I guess not!

---

73 There are more than 1,817 prophecies in the Bible. Up to now, 96.2 percent of them have already been fulfilled. (The 3.8 percent related to the end-time have yet to come to pass.) A subset of 320 prophecies about Jesus Christ has been fulfilled.

Science and Religion Can Be Reconciled!

Theoretical physicists propose models of creation according to observation and reason, or so Hawking says. The modeling is in fact a system of hypotheses to explain the observed phenomena. But the problem is that the 95 percent of the universe is invisible. So it is postulated that the invisible part of the universe is filled with dark energy and dark matter. However, their existence cannot be directly observed. Instead, models are inferred based on observations of the mysterious effects that the postulated dark matter and energy exert on the visible part of the universe (see chapter 9 on the second day of creation).

Similarly, God is a Spirit and invisible to us unless He wishes to show Himself by revelation or inspiration to believers by His sovereign choice. We can only know His presence by observing His influence on humans.

When a quantitative solution is impossible, the models are proposed by metaphysics[74] rather than by physics. When hypotheses verge closer to metaphysics than to physics, the difference between scientific and religious thought fades, and they converge into faith in God. (*We need faith to believe in science as much as in religion.* See chapter 9.)

---

74 *Metaphysics* is defined in the Merriam-Webster Dictionary as (a) a division of philosophy that is concerned with the fundamental nature of reality and being and that includes ontology, cosmology, and often epistemology; (b) abstract philosophical studies: the study of what is outside objective experience. (It is not a quantitative study like physical science.)

A Note

Finally, beloved readers, have you thought of why God led the 120-year-old Moses to walk to his own burial? Bible says that angels hid Moses' body so that nobody could find his tomb. Why?

In the eyes of the Israeli people, Moses is their greatest national hero in their history. Some people with misguided faith would probably worship him above God, by forgetting that it was God who delivered them from slavery, and Moses was only the servant of God who obeyed and carried out the physical task.

By the same token, there are many brilliant heroes in science, but they are not God. Please do remember the Ten Commandments (Exod. 20:2–17; Deut. 5:6–21), and worship only God, not science or scientists.

Please do not get me wrong. I respect and admire brilliant, humble, and godly scientists. Everybody has heard of the big bang, but only a few know the model was first proposed by a humble Catholic priest and physicist, Monsignor Georges Henri Joseph Édouard Lemaître.

In fact, I believe the big bang theory first proposed by Lemaître is a divine revelation. Why? In 1610, when Galileo publicly supported the heliocentric view of our solar system instead of the geocentric view, he met with bitter opposition from Catholic clerics. They denounced him to the Inquisition early in 1615. This time in the twentieth century, nothing seems more appropriate than for God to have revealed the big bang theory to none other than a priest of the Roman Catholic church. It cannot be coincidental; God's mercy, forgiveness, and sovereign choice are crystal clear to me.

Sir Isaac Newton, a physicist, mathematician, astronomer, natural philosopher, alchemist, and theologian, never boasted of his achievement in science. He believed that it was God who set the universe in motion, and he gave credit to scientists before him. He said, "If I have seen farther than others, it is by standing upon the shoulders of giants." He called other scientist giants. Clearly he knew and practiced the teaching of the Bible, "Do nothing from selfishness or empty conceit, but with humility of mind regard one another as more important than yourselves." (Phil. 2:3).

I believe Sir Isaac Newton earned as much respect by his faith and humility as by his scientific achievements.

The Bible teaches us that "*the fear of the LORD is the beginning of knowledge*" (Prov. 1:7). Let us learn from the Truth.

May God bless!

11. Conclusion

———————— ✌ ————————

When you have discovered a new insight in your study of the Scripture, how can you know your interpretation is intended by God?

Walter Burke, a U.S. space program general manager who must have more knowledge about outer space than us lay people, values the study of the Holy Bible and faith in the Savior. I believe he must have found life in the Scripture. For he said:

> "I have found nothing in science or space exploration to compel me to throw away my Bible or to reject my Savior Jesus Christ, in whom I trust. The space age has been a factor in the deepening of my spiritual life. I read the Bible more now. I get from the Bible what I

cannot get from science, the really important things of life." —Walter F. Burke[75]

We can see what Isaac Newton, Georges Lemaître and Walter Burke have in common—*humility*. Only to those who are humble before God does the Almighty bestow wisdom and abundant fruit.

The Lord Jesus praised the Father and said,

> I praise You, Father, Lord of heaven and earth, that You have hidden these things from the wise and intelligent and have revealed them to infants. (Matt. 11:25)

Clearly, God hides truths from the wise, intelligent, and haughty by hardening their hearts, but reveals His will to the humble. Thus the first step (I) in Bible study is to humbly ask the Holy Spirit to open our eyes and give us the wisdom we need for understanding the Scripture.

There are hidden treasures waiting for us to uncover in the Bible, especially at this time near the end of the age, when human knowledge is increasing by quantum jumps (Daniel 12:4). I believe we cannot know God's will unless He reveals it to us, and He reveals only to the extent that we can absorb it. As

---

75 W. F. Burke was a general manager of the Mercury and Gemini space programs. This quotation is from Paul Lee Tan, *Encyclopedia of 7700 Illustrations* (Maryland: Assurance Publication, 1984), 186.

human civilization progresses, the Holy Spirit will reveal more, and more clearly, from the same passage of Scripture.

Therefore, the second step (II) in Bible study is to use our God-given knowledge to observe a passage from all possible perspectives with imagination.

For example, the Lord Jesus washed His disciples' feet before eating the last supper. This event was recorded only in the Gospel of John and not in the earlier three Gospels, Matthew, Mark, and Luke. Thus, the skeptics doubt the authenticity of the event and make a career out of arguing about it. However,

- Precisely because the three earlier Gospels omitted the event, humble Christians believe that John stressed it to perfect the Bible by inspiration from God.

- Some people take this event as the Lord's teaching on *humility*, and rightly so. Because only humility enables His disciples and all His followers today to love, respect, and serve one another. The Lord, as always, is showing His teaching by example.

- In addition to humility, I believe that the Lord is also teaching *forgiveness*, *loving the unlovable*, and *loving the enemy*, for He knew that Peter was going to deny Him three times, and Judas Iscariot would soon betray Him. Yet He did not skip any one of them, but washed the feet of all twelve. Is this only my imagination?—for the Bible does not explicitly say so.

Where the treasure is not on the surface, it requires our digging. I cannot imagine that Peter would keep quiet, if Jesus had skipped him. In fact, the Scripture says that the Lord Jesus insisted on washing Peter's feet. How about Judas Iscariot? If the Lord had skipped Judas, the disciples would not have to ask who the traitor would be, when Jesus predicted that one of them would betray Him (John 13:21–25). Thus my conclusion is that Jesus washed Judas's feet as well.

- According to the Jewish custom, the disciples must have washed their hands and feet before entering the room for supper, yet the Lord washed their feet again. Why?

In addition to the teaching of humility, forgiveness, and loving the enemy, I further believe that the Lord is also teaching that people cannot cleanse themselves by just obeying the law, performing religious ceremonies, or doing good deeds alone; it is absolutely essential for our salvation that He *cleanses us of our sins by water and blood* (1 John 5:6), *by the Holy Spirit, and by fire* (Matt. 3:11).

A question naturally arises: how do we judge that our interpretation or our insight on a passage is a truth intended by God?

This question leads us to the third step (III) in Bible study—to identify whether our discovery of new insight is of human origin or is from heaven. The Bible gives us a clue in Matthew 16:13–17. Upon Peter's confession of Christ at Caesarea Philippi, the Lord says that Peter's knowledge that Jesus is the Christ has been revealed to him not by man but by the Father in Heaven.

Just as the Father was the witness to this incident, I believe we need witnesses to claim the validity of our new insights too, but how? (a) The new discovery must conform to the Scriptures, which are the words of God and His witnesses. (b) The new discovery must exalt and praise God, just as Peter's confession did. (c) The new discovery must be for the good of those who love God (Rom. 8:28). With these three witnesses, we can be assured that the new insight is *inspired* by God, so I believe.

The fourth step (IV) in Bible study is to apply the findings to our daily lives. In the above example of Jesus washing the feet of His disciples, unless we practice His teaching (not to observe the foot-washing ritual, but to love, respect, and serve one another), what good are the new insights for? To the Corinthians, Paul wrote, "Follow my example, as I follow the example of Christ" (1 Cor. 11:1, NIV).

And the Lord Jesus said,

> The kingdom of heaven is like a treasure hidden in the field, which a man found and hid again; and from joy over it he goes and sells all that he has and buys that field. (Matt. 13:44)

The Lord Jesus wants us to find the treasure (life) in the field (the Scripture) and keep it (practice it) at any cost (complete trust). He wants us to experience the joy of accepting Him, trusting and obeying His teachings, changing ourselves and growing to be more like Him day by day, to be worthy of meeting Him at last.

Beloved readers, I wish you the best in enjoying your Bible study and experiencing the joy of your closeness to our Savior Jesus Christ—a joy that not even all this world can offer!